CLASS DISMISSED

NICK ADAMS

CLASS DISMISSED

WHY COLLEGE ISN'T THE ANSWER

Post Hill
PRESS

A POST HILL PRESS BOOK

Class Dismissed:
Why College Isn't the Answer
© 2019 by Nick Adams
All Rights Reserved

ISBN: 978-1-64293-067-2
ISBN (eBook): 978-1-64293-068-9

Cover art by Cody Corcoran
Interior design and composition by Greg Johnson, Textbook Perfect

Post Hill Press
New York • Nashville
posthillpress.com

Published in the United States of America

To the American Originals, the dreamers,
the men who saw into the future and made it a reality.
Your legacy lives on and continues to inspire
new generations of Americans to reach for the stars.

INTRODUCTION

My father, Andrew, was a mathematics teacher at Christian Brothers Fellowship in Sydney, Australia. He taught math to the Australian equivalent of American high school seniors. Despite the fact that Aussies have a reputation for being kind, wonderful, good-hearted, cheerful, and hilarious, my father would often get in arguments with his students.

The topics in question: college; careers. *The future.*

In addition to teaching very gifted, very polished kids—kids who nailed their exams; kids who wore suits and ties to school; kids who were quite good at saying, "Yes, sir" and "Yes, ma'am" when it was called for—my father also had students who weren't that hot in math. Sometimes these not-so-good students would tell dad that they were planning on becoming a doctor, or a lawyer, or pursuing a well-paying, high-level, white collar career. Sort of a champagne taste on a *plonk* budget!

Dad, being a nice guy, would tell his students as tactfully as he could that maybe doctoring or lawyering wasn't a logical path, that maybe they should aim in a different direction. Not a dumbed-down direction, mind you, just different. His thinking was, if these kids were struggling with the level of math he was teaching them, their chances of succeeding in college pursuing high-minded careers were probably quite slim.

Even as a kid, I thought his approach was pretty cool.

Sometimes the kids would just end the conversation there, but once in a while, they'd get into a back-and-forth with dad, and he would say, "Look, if I had it to do all over again, I would probably go and be a plumber."

At that point, the student would say, "Um, what?"

That's a fair, logical reaction. As far as the students were concerned, Dad was a successful teacher. He was respected. He was probably making a nice salary. On one memorable occasion, a student blurted out, "You'd rather be a plumber? Bullshit!"

Dad would generally say something along the lines of, "Yeah, I would have been a plumber or an electrician, but I would've preferred to be a plumber. See, the worst thing that I could do in plumbing was flood somebody's house. But if I'm an electrician, and I'm no good, I might end up electrocuting someone... or myself. With plumbing, the stakes are a little bit lower." (All legitimate points. My father is nothing if not practical.)

Unsurprisingly, the school administration didn't take kindly to those particular conversations. That's a fair reaction, because if you're the principal of any school, you're measured in part by the success of your students. If your students don't go to college, but rather take up a trade—especially a trade like plumbing that some might perceive as less than noble or impressive—well, you might not come off as the best school leader in the world.

The parents who heard about these conversations weren't thrilled either. They'd ring up the harried principal and complain that my father was killing the dreams of their tender children. Few parents want to have a teacher tell their child that they're not cut out for college, and that they should consider becoming a plumber or an electrician.

Gasp! Oh my goodness! Heaven forbid that honesty (or plumbing) enter into the equation!

The whole idea is that taking up a trade like that—being a plumber, or an electrician, or a carpenter, or a welder, or a machinist, or doing any occupation that involves working with your hands—is a fall from grace.

That's understandable. That makes sense. After all, the Moms and Dads of the world are spending all this money to get their child educated at this good private school, and to them, a career in plumbing isn't a good return on a large investment. The parents want the child to be better than they are, to head off to college, to take on a high-profile job, to make a ton of money, to have loads of status in the community.

And let's be honest: it is, to some extent, about the parents. If the child goes to college and lands a law or medical degree, the mother and father can tell their friends and family, "Boy, we raised that kid right. He's got a good salary. She lives in a nice house. He has a nice car. She has a vacation home by the beach." Another reason: they don't want to hear about fixing leaky pipes.

Fair enough. But here's the thing. When you're visiting a doctor or a lawyer, it's usually not for something good. You very rarely hear somebody saying, "I have an appointment with my attorney because I just won eight-million dollars in the Powerball lottery, and I need to figure out how to maximize my wealth without getting thrown in jail." It's generally more along the lines of, "I just got sued for plowing into a parked car, and my lawyer needs to help me not lose all my money in the lawsuit."

I don't know about you, but if somebody wants to haul me into court, I want my lawyer to be really good, really smart, and really slick. And if my lawyer is a guy whose high school math teacher told him, "You're not college material," that might not be the lawyer of my dreams.

And what about doctors? If there's even the slightest chance that my general practitioner barely skated by in high school... *and* college...*and* medical school, that's not a good thing either. If Dr. What's-His-Name was a mediocre student, he might well be a mediocre doctor, and I don't want to get poked or prodded by a mediocre doctor.

All of which is why the entire continent of Australia owes my father a hearty thank you.

This isn't strictly an Australian issue—kids who shouldn't be attending college actually attending college. This is a problem throughout the world, especially in the United States.

It's an issue that I think about all the time.

Why? Why do I mull over the educational system? I'm not currently teaching. As of this writing, I don't have any children. I went to a great college. I earned two degrees, and nabbed my bachelor's degree in two years, rather than four.

Not only did I do well in college, I bloody loved it! But how could I not? I went from a private, all-boys boarding school that was very strict with lots of rules and limitations on language and behavior and clothing to a school where I could do whatever I wanted. University classes were all fine and good—I was always a good student, so there wasn't much in the way of stress—but my goodness, I loved the social antics. That was the real paperweight for me; that kept things interesting, even when the classes got dull.

Not only that, but my college education tangibly added *something* to me. Even today, I can't tell you exactly what that *something* is—something like that is almost impossible to quantify because often, you don't even realize the effect that *something* has on you until months or years, or decades later. But it's *something*.

This I can say for certain: college put me on the path that led me to this moment in my life—a moment in which I can make my living without having to report to a boss; a moment in which I can write an entire book on a topic about which I'm completely passionate and completely invested; a moment in which I have the opportunity to give speeches all over the country: speeches about society, and politics, and the American Dream.

Please note that when I write "American Dream," that capital "D" is there for a reason.

I went to the University of Sydney in the early 2000s. (University of Sydney, it should be noted, is kind of the Harvard in Australia.) Colleges, whether they're located in Australia, or America, or the South Pole, were different then, especially from a political perspective. Back then, a conservative and a liberal could always have a civil discussion about the state of the world. (Okay, not *always*. But certainly more often than now. Today, the polarization between belief systems is outrageous. It's hard to find a common ground.)

When I started school, I wasn't that interested in politics anyway (ironic considering who and what I've become). I just went through college like any other young man, and built my own social circle, and had a great amount of fun, and simply loved it.

I was free to find out who I was, and what I wanted to be, and where I fit in society. For me, the great benefit was that I was exposed to different social circles, different groups, different types of people from rural areas, people from urban areas. So, yeah, I began to really find my feet in society.

I was there for a reason. I was college material.

I'm not bragging or boasting. It was just a fact. I had good study habits, I got good grades, and I legitimately enjoyed education. If I wasn't good in school (or maybe even if I was) and I was living in the United States, a country that has a more pro-business atmosphere than Australia—I'd have skipped college in a heartbeat. You see, American culture is built for the entrepreneur, the young hotshot who wants to think outside the box and color outside the lines. If I were in America, I wouldn't have even thought twice—I'd have gone down the entrepreneurial route immediately.

Because isn't that the American Dream?

America is a place where kids get the most opportunity and the most freedom to go out and pursue whatever they want to pursue. This is the country with the least judgmental attitude, the place it's very clear that people care the least about your reputation. Here in America, if you go sell spa baths and you make twenty-five million dollars a year, or if you make one hundred thousand dollars hawking party balloons, nobody will dismiss you because you're not a doctor or a lawyer. You don't have to be ashamed of how you made the money, because, simply put: *you made the money.*

That being the case, the American Dream definitely doesn't involve college. American originals like Walt Disney, Henry Ford, Steve Jobs, and Bill Gates didn't need a full complement of higher education to succeed. They needed their creativity and their highly original skill sets. Maybe they knew the American Dream was never about going to college, or maybe they didn't, but either way, they didn't care. Their American Dream was about being inventive and creative, having genius, and marketing skills, and the ability to sell yourself and your product, and the drive to push and hustle, regardless of the obstacle.

I firmly believe this is the only country in the world where failure is not fatal, where you can fall down five thousand times and get up five thousand and one. If you've got great determination and tenacity, you'll eventually be just fine.

Because this is the only country in the world where you can blaze a trail and leave a legacy.

This is the only country in the world where you can color outside the lines and not be punished.

This is the only country in the world where success is not resented, but rather admired and aspired to.

This is the only country in the world where your first language or last name means absolutely nothing.

This is the only country in the world where you can rise above your circumstances and achieve whatever you want to achieve.

And no matter what anybody tells you, you don't need a traditional education to make it happen.

Let me say that again, except louder: *you don't need a traditional education to make it happen!*

All you need is self-confidence, passion, a rugged determination, a one-track mind that insists you are going to do whatever it takes to succeed, and the energy to make it all possible. You've got to work very hard for as long as it's going to take, and eventually you're going to get there. That's the great story. Think about it: Walt Disney went bankrupt twice. Henry Ford went bankrupt twice. Thomas Edison had a thousand cracks at the light bulb before he finally got it to work. Colonel Sanders had his fried chicken recipe rejected one thousand and nine times before he got a "yes." But they fulfilled their respective dreams, and that, my friends, is the American way.

Admittedly, diving into the business world at a young age without a diploma in your back pocket isn't easy. But if that's the direction you choose to go—and you have a plan, and the energy, and all that good stuff—*it will work out.*

You just have to understand what you know, and what you're good at, and what you love, and what you're passionate about. And you've got to be realistic. For instance, if you struggled with fractions and you want to handle the bookkeeping at the café you intend to open, well, you might want to find somebody else to deal with the bank deposits. Another example: If your English skills aren't great, if you can't write a good essay, if you consistently earned Cs on your essays, you probably should find somebody else to handle the social media for your theoretical café. If you're not good at speaking in public, get somebody else to pitch your café to investors.

But if you can bake, and you know how to make a room look pleasing to the eye, and you're passionate about coffee, *screw college.* Write a business proposal, find investors, and *open the bloody café.*

You have to be really honest with yourself about what you're good at, and no matter what you think, no matter what your high school grades were (or are), no matter what anybody tells you, *you are good at something.*

You see, everyone is good at something. Everyone has a place. Everyone has a talent. Unfortunately, though, the way that our culture has been sectioned, we've encouraged some people to bury their natural talents and instead go to college, where they're led down a different path; where they are often told to embrace the thing at which they're mediocre. I mean, imagine how many English literature majors wanted nothing to do with books. I shudder to think.

I feel all of this boils down to whether you want mediocrity or greatness. I believe it's a path to mediocrity if you're going to slog your way through college when you could have gone out and become a great welder and eventually launched a firm where you employed other welders and became an entrepreneur.

That's showing your full potential, and America is all about showing your full potential, right? It's about throwing off the shackles of the norm. You don't have to follow the crowd to the University of Wherever, where you'll trudge through your classes and graduate (barely) without a true direction, without a skill set that can help you earn a quality living. You might also graduate with a six-figure debt to your name.

Another obstacle in realizing the dream of self-sufficiency, of independence, and of an entrepreneurial life is your family.

Now don't get me wrong. If you're reading this book, chances are you're either a high schooler who's wrestling with the decision as to whether or not to continue your education in a traditional manner—and I say traditional manner, because attending a trade school is a huge non-traditional option that will be discussed in great detail later on—or you're a parent who has a child that might not be college material, and you're afraid to admit to the child or yourself that college isn't the best decision.

Both of you—the high school student and the parent—want what's best for everybody.

Everybody's goal is a lifetime of happiness, health, and success. But for the last few generations, college has been considered the first and biggest step towards reaching that goal. And a goodly number of parents who've had that drilled into their head don't want to think outside the box.

The family belief that a college degree is the best, indeed the only way to make it in this world, has been ingrained in many of us—thus the familial pressure. I think it's more amplified here in the United States, because there is an aspirational quality to American society. I *love* that quality, and I don't for one second suggest it should be in any way diminished. This aspirational quality sets Americans apart from every other culture in the world, and it makes Americans part of the best culture.

Having said that, what we need is the *right kind of aspiration*. When a parent wants their kid to go to college because they didn't, well, it's understandable. I get that. But it's really not the right way to approach things. You don't do something—*anything*—just because you've been told time and again that it's the right thing to do. You don't make a decision based on everybody else's decisions.

Anecdotally speaking, I feel that this is an issue particularly conflicting to non-college-graduate parents who have blue-collar jobs. They look at their career and think, *I want my kid to do better than me. I want my kid to make more money than I made. I want my kid to change the world, and people who skip college aren't world-changers.*

Wrong.

Your child *can* change the world without a piece of sheepskin. Your child *can* change the world without wearing a suit and tie. Your child *can* have a brilliant life by nurturing what they're best at, not what the world tells them (and you) should be nurtured.

All of which is why I took the time to write forty thousand-or-so words about this topic. With these forty thousand words, I'm going to tell you my story, and you'll understand why I've grown so passionate about alternatives to a traditional education.

With these forty thousand words, I'm going to discuss many, many different educational options that will hopefully lead you on a path to a fulfilled soul and a decent bank account.

With these forty thousand words, I'm going to introduce you to some people who bucked the trends, who took a non-standard, sometimes circuitous route to a quality life.

And after reading these forty thousand words, my hope is that you can feel comfortable about making the decision about your or your family's education that's best for you.

1

Right now, you might be asking yourself, "Why the hell would a guy who had such a wonderful college experience spend all this time writing forty thousand words about why you don't need college?"

Well, there's no short answer to that question, so strap in for the long one.

I worked really, really hard in high school. I studied even when I didn't necessarily need to. It was impressed upon me from a very early age by my parents that the most important thing, the number one priority for me, was to do well academically, and I really applied myself throughout elementary, middle, and high school.

In college, oddly enough, I didn't have to apply myself quite as much. The academic stuff came easily to me. Turns out I happen to be one of those people who's really lucky, and fortunate, and blessed in that it'll take me an hour of studying to do what others might need a full day to absorb.

I remember one time I was sitting in a history class and a friend told me rather proudly that he had taken seventeen hours over the weekend to study for our history quiz. Now, the quiz in question wasn't a particularly important one—it wasn't a midterm or a final, just a mid-semester check-up—and he asked me how long I'd spent prepping.

I shrugged and said, "Gosh, maybe an hour."

He looked less than pleased.

So the quiz happened, and he correctly answered seventeen out of the thirty questions. He was, quite simply, devastated. I, on the other hand, managed to nail twenty-seven out of thirty. I don't tell you this to brag or boast, just to illustrate how lucky I am that my mind works the way my mind works. (Parents, I'm not saying your child needs to have a quirky brain like mine to be considered college material. I'm also not saying that if your child has a quirky brain, they should automatically attend college. Keep in mind as you read this book that these decisions should be made on a case-by-case basis. There's no specific right and no specific wrong, just what's best for the specific teenager headed into adulthood.)

My friend, of course, thought that was very unfair, and he sputtered, "But…but…you…but…you…didn't…but…"

I could certainly understand his perspective.

There were other plusses about university as opposed to high school. High school was about conformity. My school—an elite private school—was very stuffy, full of rules, about, well, *everything*. If your shoes weren't polished, you were put on what was called a dress parade, the less about which is said, the better. If you didn't roll your sleeves up above your elbows, that was a detention. If you didn't have your tie properly done up, that was a big ol' no-no.

College offered me the freedom and the ability to really become who I wanted to become. There were no constraints.

There wasn't a blueprint. There was just my quirky brain and me.

Before I started university, I wasn't particularly excited. I never lay awake at night, dreaming of a college education—or, for that matter, a college experience. But that all changed quickly. Right off the bat, I loved college.

I loved how I was able to come into my own. I loved how I was able to do things *my* way. I loved that I could be an independent learner if I so chose. I loved that I could work out my own schedule and not have somebody checking in on me every five minutes, be they a teacher or a parent.

That's when Nick Adams became Nick Adams.

Quicker than I could've imagined, I got a really good feel for who I was, for what I believed in, what my dreams were, where my passions lay, what I didn't like, the kind of people I wanted to hang around with and have in my life, and the kind of people I *didn't* want to hang around with and have in my life. (Having said all that, college isn't necessary in terms of helping you find yourself. A friend of mine skipped college and headed right into the work force, and while he told me that college would have offered him a better shot at getting laid—his word, not mine—he wouldn't have become the person he became without the friendships and business relationships he developed on the job. And he ended up marrying the woman of his dreams—a woman he met on the job—so it had a happy ending all around. The only group that wasn't happy was whatever school would have otherwise taken his tuition.)

My days at college were incredible. When I think about the various phases of my life, the joyous freedom and the (relative) lack of responsibility that one has at college is hard to beat. It was a time to thrive, and I realized when I was at college that I had a very unique gift—the ability to communicate and relate to people totally unlike me. By coming into contact with the wide variety of individuals at school, I learned that I could easily converse and befriend anybody, regardless of their level of intellect. I could speak to, say, a potential Supreme Court Justice with as much enthusiasm and fulfillment as I could speak to the guy cleaning the toilets at night. You see, I don't look down on anybody, regardless of a person's lot in life. That's probably one of the reasons I'm such a proponent of alternate routes, post-high school. It doesn't matter what you do—it's how you do it and who you are *while* you're doing it. If the Supreme Court Justice is a jerk who's horrible at his job, I'll be considerably less interested in bonding with him than I would with the good-natured, good-hearted, diligent toilet-cleaner.

Admittedly, I didn't make the most of my college years. I didn't study anywhere nearly as hard as I should have, and if somebody felt like being particularly harsh, they would say I wasted a gift; that I squandered the intellect for academic study I'd been given. This is something to consider when somebody is on the fence as to whether college is the right choice—whether or not they'll make the most of the opportunity. If they're not going to study, there's little logic in utilizing all that money and time. Not a good investment, eh?

Why didn't I study as much as I should have? Well, aside from the fact that I did relatively well *with little study*, I was distracted by the social life. I'm far from the only person in this world who got swept up by the social life. All over the campus (all over the world) there are kids who—away from home for the first time—go off the rails and wash out of school.

Eventually, I figured out a system, a unique approach to school that worked for me. (The operative phrase there is "for me." My system isn't for everybody. For that matter, some might say that my system isn't for *anybody*.) I'm not necessarily proud of this, but at college, once I worked out how it all functioned, I figured out a routine that offered me more time to have fun.

In my school, there were lectures and there were tutorials. Now, with tutorials you can only miss one or two, but if you're regularly absent, you don't pass the course. With lectures, conversely, nobody takes attendance. So, I realized very quickly that lectures were an expendable part of my timetable, while tutorials were not.

That said, lectures were a very important part of the actual educational process, so I would use my wiles to find somebody who I knew, or who I charmed within the first couple of minutes of class, to get them to take notes for the lectures for me. I'd get the information, and I'd save the time. (Even though it worked for me, I don't endorse this approach. If that's the way you or your child plans to attack college, why bother?)

It should be noted that I didn't completely ignore lectures. The first week of the semester, I would go to both the lecture *and* the tutorial because I needed to get the assignments and the test dates. Once I worked out those logistics, *that's* when I'd try and find a kind soul who would get me those notes.

Another one of my tricks was when I was at a tutorial, I made sure I was the first student to say something, because if you were the first one to talk, it was likely that you wouldn't get called on again. So I would say something rather innocuous, then let things progress. The teachers thought I was on the same page as the rest of the class because I'd initiated the conversation.

That was the Nick Adams approach to school—very adaptable—and while it worked smashingly for me, I wouldn't recommend it to anybody—I would certainly never want my future children to follow the same path—but that's what I did and I don't have any regrets because I am really exactly where I wanted to be, and my life really turned out the way I wanted it to.

The interesting thing is that before I evolved into who and what I wanted to be, I figured I'd become an attorney, which, in Australia, is the summit, the zenith, the tippy-top of the top professions. It's not that I had a particular passion for the law. I just figured that being at the summit, the zenith, and the tippy-top would mean a life of absurd wealth. And when you're of a certain age—like, say, fourteen—absurd wealth is what it's all about.

But the legal world wasn't in the cards for me. I ended up doing media communications, and thank God for that, because that was a far better use of my skill set. For those of you who know me, you might be saying to yourself, "But Nick, you might be the perfect guy to speak in front of a jury. You're outgoing, you like to talk; you're pretty darn good at communicating with people from all walks of life. I'd probably let you represent me in my murder trial."

Maybe that's true, and maybe not, but the fact of the matter is that the vast majority of lawyers aren't trial lawyers. They're patent lawyers, or bankruptcy lawyers, or intellectual property lawyers, lawyers who wear suits, and sit behind desks, and are overworked and underpaid and over-caffeinated…and probably have a pile of student loans from both undergrad and graduate school that need paying back.

Here's another interesting Nick Adams College Fact: while I was at school—in my second year, just eight days after I turned twenty-one—I was elected to public office. Not student council. Public office. Yours truly was one of the youngest councilmen in Australian history. And not too long thereafter, I became the youngest deputy mayor in the Sydney area in the history of Australia. (Needless to say, what with the media attention, the on-the-job learning, and serving the public to the best of my ability, my political life put a crimp in my studies.)

Right now, you might be wondering if I would've won these elections without being able to say I was currently studying at the University of Sydney. Truthfully, not attending college at that time probably would have counted against me. I'm not saying I would have lost the race, because elections tend to be about knocking on doors, meeting with people, and selling yourself and your vision and your abilities to them. Certainly it impressed people that I was so studious and conscientious, that I was not only studying at university, but that I wanted to serve the public and help people and do something else, which is rare for a nineteen-year-old college student. Because, you know, nineteen-year-old college students tend to be having the time of their life, with little interest in anything else.

Nobody thought I would win that first election. I was told that it would be like banging my head against a wall, and that the best I could hope for was that it would be a good experience and it would go on the curriculum vitae, and the political party would be grateful to me in the future and look favorably upon me when the time came for me to actually run for something I could win. Truth be told, I was the only person who actually believed I could win. Being the self-starter that I am, I went and knocked on every door twice and got elected—all of which dovetails into my dream of being a motivational speaker.

Good politicians want to do good things. They want to help people. They want to make a difference. These are all qualities that make for a quality motivational speaker.

Backtracking for a moment, during my freshman orientation week, I ran into one of my fellow students—a kid I knew in high school who was four years my senior—who had become involved in politics. He sold me on joining the conservative club on campus. (It wasn't just the politics that sucked me in. He told me there were lots of social functions with lots of cheap beer, so I gave it a go.) One thing led to another, and slowly but surely, I was injected with the political drug.

I'm fond of saying that if that had not happened, if those particular people had not been put in my path, if I hadn't have fallen into this oddball variety of situations, who knows where I would have landed? As a believer in God, I love Billy Preston's song, "That's The Way God Planned It." Why? Well, the song explains why we should be humble, and asks why there's so much greediness in this world, and tells us that we should treat each other with kindness and respect, and…ah, just go ahead and download it. It's awesome.

2

I'm convinced that if I had I not been injected with that political drug, I would have focused solely on becoming a straight up, no nonsense motivational speaker. I mean, I'd listened to motivational speakers for as long as I can remember: Les Brown, Tony Robbins, and Zig Ziglar—all of the big guys. I've read their books and a ton of others, so it's in my bloodstream.

(A quick tangent: another thing I love about the United States is that so many people are open to self-help. That's not the case at all with most Australians. Self-help isn't really a big thing Down Under. There isn't this hunger for success and this thirst to make bank and do well and succeed. People out there just like to coast. They like to have a good life, to own a good home, to make a good salary, to be able to buy all the beer that they want, to be able to buy all the food that they want, to be able to swing on the porch, and that's it. There's nothing wrong with that, necessarily—I like swinging on the porch with a beer as much as the next guy—but I wanted more.)

And for a young man like me, a kid who had all of these grand ambitions, I was more interested in developing myself and teaching myself, the same way I'd been doing my whole life, even all the way back in elementary and middle school, when I'd read Thesauruses, or scour through foreign language books *just because*.

I've always had that kind of self-starting attitude, an attitude that I think is built into the American DNA. I, like a huge percentage of Americans, have an insatiable appetite for progress, for innovation, for *more*.

I've always wanted more. Always.

Not only did I want more, I wanted other people to have more, and I wanted to find a way to give it to them. That's why inspiration and motivation are things that really appeal to me.

To that end, I love watching *America's Got Talent*. I hated it at first, and my then-fiancé and now-wife made me stick with it. She'd say, "This really should be right up your alley because the overwhelming majority of these contestants are all dreamers. They're people from all over the country who have spent all of their money just to come to the biggest stage on television to possibly win *America's Got Talent*; to be discovered. And that's you to a 'T.'"

At that point, I started *really* watching it, and when I heard all of the stories and explanations that people would give when they first took the stage when answering the judges' questions, I was kind of blown away: "Do you know why you are here? What is your end goal? What is your dream? Where do you want to go?"

Their answers were uniformly inspiring, whether they were looking to overcome a difficult upbringing or simply let the world hear them sing.

This explains why *Rocky* is one of my favorite movies. In case you haven't seen it, it's about Rocky Balboa, a boxer who got knocked down time and again, and never failed to attempt to get up. He didn't always make it up, mind you, but he tried. (It should be noted that Rocky never went to college, and he did pretty well for himself. Sure, he's a fictional character, but you get the point.)

This explains why hearing a story about, say, a man who lived in his car for two years before becoming a successful *whatever* moves me more than anything.

This explains why I'm inspired to inspire.

I want to make sure that every American and the generations to come have the most opportunity and the most confidence to achieve and pursue their dreams. I want to make sure that every American is equipped with the confidence and with the opportunity to go out there and realize the dreams that are in their heart. All of us have dreams. Every single one of us. And they're all legitimate. You just need to find a way to realize them.

And those dreams don't necessarily need a college education.

I don't have the numbers to back this up—no numbers can back this one up, frankly—but it feels to me that 99 percent of us, well, we settle. We look at our circumstances, and think, "I'm doing okay. I'm paying the bills. I have a decent place to live. Sure, I spend 60 hours of my week at this job I don't love, and if I'm awake for about 112 hours a week, that means I'm not loving my life for over half of my existence, but that's fine, that's good enough."

See? Settling.

Far too many of us don't have the confidence to take the leap, to take the risk. In writing this book, I hope to encourage students and Americans of all stripes to take that leap. For centuries, entrepreneurship has been the path and the dream for people coming to this country and for people living in this country. Everything is made for the success of the individual in this country. This is the only country where failure is not fatal.

Sure, it's scary to go against the grain and skip college. You're crazy if you don't think that forgoing a college degree—something for which Americans have strived since Harvard University was founded in 1636—is an easy decision.

I'm not a huge basketball fan, but there are a couple of quotes from NBA players that have stuck with me:

> "I've missed more than nine thousand shots in my career. I've lost almost three hundred games. Twenty-six times I've been trusted to take the game winning shot and missed. I've failed over and over and over again in my life. And that is why I succeed."
>
> —MICHAEL JORDAN

> "If I fall down seven times, I'll get up eight."
>
> —DWYANE WADE

That's why Michael Jordan is in the NBA Hall of Fame. That's why Dwyane Wade will someday be in the NBA Hall of Fame.

This attitude is something that's unique to America; it really is. This is what America is all about: *having* chances and *taking* chances. It's the land of ceaseless opportunity—provided you are willing to seize it. What I want to do is give people the confidence to go out there and achieve it, whether or not that involves college.

As strange as it may seem, part of that little plan of mine involves instilling a little bit of fear.

Actually, instilling a *lot* of fear.

3

As noted in the very first paragraph of this book, Australians have a reputation for being kind, wonderful, good-hearted, cheerful, and hilarious. I'd like to think that I'm as kind, wonderful, good-hearted, cheerful, and hilarious as the next Aussie.

All of which is why it saddens me that I have to spend an entire chapter scaring the crap out of you.

Listen, college is intrinsically scary in and of itself. It's a child's first time living on their own—heck, in some cases, it's their first time away from the house on their own for any significant amount of time. I don't have facts and figures on this one, but if I were to guesstimate, I'd say that 361 percent of all college freshman are really, really nervous for much of their first semester. That's right, 361 percent. Maybe 362 percent.

And that's fair. That's understandable. The beginning of adulthood is frightening—but it *should* be frightening in a *constructive* manner. A teenager should be able to take that fear and translate it into fuel—entrepreneurial fuel; fuel to make a positive societal impact; fuel to succeed beyond *anybody's* wildest dreams.

Fuel to change the world.

In any event, this chapter falls under the category of opening your mind, of dropping knowledge, of helping you prepare to make the biggest decision of you or your child's young life... and, of course, of scaring the crap out of you. To that end, here are a few topics of which you should be aware before writing the University of Wherever an often useless six-figure check:

There is too Much F****** Political Correctness on Campus!

Some might say there's too much political correctness *off* campus, but that particular topic merits a book of its own.

In her article for the *National Review* titled "The 16 Most Ridiculously PC Moments on College Campuses in 2016," Katherine Timpf reeled off a list of PC for-instances that rubbed me the wrong way. For example, there was the Harvard student's declaration that a bench can be a racial issue. This particularly misguided young man wrote that "...[everything] is about race. Our country was built on oppression, and race is everywhere, at every moment on my standard trip back to Harvard."

Calm down, my Harvard friend, just calm down. Seriously, you'd think an Ivy Leaguer would be a bit more earthbound.

And then there's Southwestern University in Texas, who cancelled a performance of "The Vagina Monologues" because the play was *written by a white woman*. Regardless of how you feel about the work, it should be allowed to be produced without anybody complaining.

This is becoming a worldwide thing. Even at Oxford University—Oxford, dear readers, *Oxford*—students weren't taught about rape because the administration believed said knowledge would be "a trigger."

Come on, people. I've read the Constitution—all the amendments, especially the first one. It's absurd for a family to invest in four years of this astoundingly counterproductive brainwashing…brainwashing that nobody has to worry about if a student jumps right from high school into the work force.

Segregation is a Thing

In 2017, as described by TheRoot.com, Harvard University held a separate graduation ceremony that was open only to black graduate students. This wasn't the school's decision—*it was the students' decision*. And this group of black students was so dead-set on making it happen that they crowd-funded the whole damn thing.

So, I ask all the teenagers reading this, is that the way you want to launch into the next phase of your adulthood? Do you want to go to a place where many of your fellow students are so filled with alienation and anger that they insist on separating themselves from you? What kind of lesson does that teach? How does that help prepare you for your professional life?

The answers: no; no; a lousy one; and it doesn't.

Sure, you'll stumble across some intolerant-types at your post-high-school job, but the chances of this sort of attitude being thrown in your face, Harvard-style, are slim.

And then there's the 2016 article from ABC News that discusses the segregated housing at California State University, which the school administration described as a "themed living community." A themed living community? How could any self-respecting public relations flack write that kind of tripe without getting nauseous?

These are harmful situations to all students, regardless of their race or creed. If a college graduate is thrust into the real world with the belief that this kind of negativity is okay, well, all I can say is that's engendering a sense of hate that will take years to counteract.

And *these* specific lessons taught in *these* specific manners would *never* be delivered to the high school graduate had the college attendee in question *not* been a college attendee.

Colleges are Sketchy About Money

CollegeBoard.org tells us that the 2017–2018 average in-state tuition at a state public university was 9,970 dollars; the average out-of-state public university tuition was 25,620 dollars; and the average private school tuition was 34,740 dollars. On top of that, the National Center for Education Statistics said that in the fiscal year 2015, United States universities received a total of 547 billion dollars in endowments.

That's a whole lot of money.

One would assume that said money would go towards, y'know, education, and teaching, and learning resources.

One's assumption is often wrong.

To wit: in a 2018 piece called "How Rich Universities Waste Their Endowments," *Washington Monthly* detailed (as one might logically surmise from the title) how rich universities waste their endowments. Between 2011-2017, for example, the University of Texas at Austin received 603 million dollars of endowments from an oil company, only 143 million dollars of which was used on general administration, and only 38 dollars million of which was used for financial aid.

Some quick addition—addition that can be done without a college education, thank you very much—tells us that we have 422 million dollars that was delivered to *who the hell knows where*?

So not only do we have another situation where the lesson taught to the students is one of negativity, but it's also fair to assume that some of the students' 9,970 dollars, or 25,620 dollars, or 34,740 dollars is *also* going to *who the hell knows where*.

One thing we *do* know is that there are a whole bunch of college administrators who have some questionably large bank accounts. Which begs the question: do you really want to give your hard-earned money to a corrupt administration?

Yeah, me neither.

Finally, there's New York's Colgate University, a place that, according to a 2017 *Forbes* article called "U.S. Colleges: Where Does the Money Go?" receives so many endowments that the school can survive by charging students a relatively reasonable tuition of 14,500 dollars.

This is opposed to Colgate's *actual* annual average tuition of 62,540 dollars.

More money lining more undeserving pockets. Appalling. Simply appalling.

All of this—the over-the-top political correctness, the separation of students, and the overt corruption—is enough to break my kind, wonderful, good-hearted, cheerful, and hilarious Aussie heart.

It should be enough to make *you* reconsider the value, the logic, and the wisdom of sinking tens of thousands of dollars into a higher education.

4

(Author's note: if you aren't a fan of facts, figures, and statistics—if you prefer the more personal touch—feel free to skip to the next chapter. I won't be upset.)

Before I continue telling the Nick Adams story and how it relates to whether or not a student, circa the late 2010s, should go to college, let's hear from some people with hardcore educational credentials, like Jeffrey Selingo.

More than three million students will graduate from U.S. high schools this month, and two-thirds of them will head off to college next fall. If history is any guide, for many of them, their high school graduation might be their last commencement ceremony. Fewer than 40 percent of students enrolling for the first time at a four-year college graduate in four years. Add in community colleges, and more than half of students who start college drop out within six years.

That's what Selingo, author of *There is Life After College: What Parents and Students Should Know about Navigating School to Prepare for the Jobs of Tomorrow*, wrote in the *New York Post* in June 2018. Selingo went on to say that, "Most problematic was who finished and who did not: Basically, wealthy students graduated, and low-income students did not. Children from families earning more than 90,000 dollars have a 1-in-2 chance of getting a bachelor's degree by twenty-four. That falls to a one in seventeen chance for families earning under 35,000 dollars."

That's some disconcerting stuff.

Selingo also told the story of David Laude, a chemistry professor and senior vice provost at the University of Texas at Austin,

> While many campuses have recently started to do something to improve student learning and outcomes, Laude was an early convert. In the late 1990s, Laude was teaching an introductory chemistry course at UT-Austin, like he had been since 1987. Over the course of a few years, however, he noticed the distribution of grades in his classes was shifting… Of the five hundred students in his class, about four hundred were on one side with As and Bs. The rest were at the bottom, with Ds and Fs. Few were in the middle…Laude wanted to try something different. In fall 1999, he pulled fifty students from his five-hundred-seat chemistry class who came from low-income families, from families whose parents did not go to college, or who had low SAT scores. He enrolled them in a smaller fifty-seat class he taught right after the larger class.

Quoting Laude, Selingo continued,

> 'It was the same material, it was just as hard, but I changed my attitude about these students,' he said. 'We beat into their heads that they were scholars, that they were great.' In addition, he assigned these students advisers and peer mentors. When the semester was over, the students in the smaller class had achieved the same grades as those in the larger

section...In the following years, Laude's approach was replicated in biology and calculus courses...So far, their efforts seem to be working. Data released last year show the university's four-year graduation rate rose from 52 percent in 2013 to 66 percent in 2017, and the growth spanned racial groups and family income levels.

That's an inspiring story—and you know I appreciate an inspiring story—but there are two major holes: one, a 66 percent graduation rate still means that one out of three students will wash out without delivering a return on their and their family's considerable financial and time investment, and two, there aren't that many David Laudes in the educational system.

The point being, a college may have the best intentions, but the chances of injecting an uninspired student with enough inspiration to thrive and embrace school—let alone make it through four years—is relatively slim. Again, it's on a case-by-case basis, but that 33 percent should give you—the parent who wants to shove their child into college, or the kid who is the one being shoved—a whole lot of pause.

While my particular take on the necessity (or lack thereof) of college isn't at all mainstream, there are still some educators who are on my side. In 2015, Jillian Gordon, a public school teacher in Ohio, wrote a treatise for *pbs.org* titled, "Why I'm Telling Some of My Students Not to Go to College."

Jillian, you had me at hello.

Gordon wrote,

I tell many of my students not to go to a four-year college. Many of you are gasping at this point, I'm sure. But with student loan debt reaching an all-time high of 1.2 trillion dollars (surpassing credit card debt), and little research to support that the investment is worth it, I am cheating my student by not encouraging them to make the best choice for themselves. And a four-year degree is not always synonymous with 'best choice.'

(This bit goes out to those of you who, at some point while reading this book, have said or will say, "Come on, Nick, you're not an academic. Why should we listen to your take on college?")

Gordon then delivered an anecdote that my father—you remember, the math teacher who told his students that they should consider skipping university—will appreciate:

A few years ago, I worked closely with a student who very much wanted to be a reporter. She was passionate about it, and spoke about her dreams with wide eyes and a contagious smile. The issue? This student's writing was subpar at best, and her talents, while immense, were not shown through her academic ability. She simply did not have the grades to make it through four more years of college. Guilty of it myself, I watched as all of her teachers smiled at her and encouraged her to follow her dreams, no one having the courage to push in her a direction that was more logical for her to take. We smiled and watched as she dropped out of college and moved back home with no back-up plan in place.

In researching this book, I read numerous iterations of this story, some of which had a more positive outcome. For instance, the story of Garret Morgan, which aired on *All Things Considered* in summer 2018:

Like most other American high school students, Garret Morgan had it drummed into him constantly: Go to college.

Get a bachelor's degree. "All through my life it was, 'if you don't go to college you're going to end up on the streets,'" Morgan said. "Everybody's so gung-ho about going to college."

Morgan gave it a shot, and it didn't stick, so he decided to pivot. That pivot? Ironwork. Once he completed his ironworker training, he was brought on full-time and got benefits, including a pension. At the time of this writing, Morgan was earning 28.36 dollars an hour, or more than fifty thousand dollars a year, which is almost certain to steadily increase. The story went on to say, "As for his friends from high school, 'they're still in college,' he said with a wry grin. 'Someday maybe they'll make as much as me.'"

In her aforementioned article, Jillian Gordon posited,

I had to learn the hard way that sometimes it's our jobs as teachers to tell students no, otherwise life will do it for them—and life is rarely ready to catch them when they fall. We are doing a disservice to our students. We are assuming all students need the same thing: that they need to go to college. When we know that it may not be the best choice for them, we are cheating them of reality and a worthy, challenging education simply because they are the textbook version of a 'good student.' We do not have the courage to tell them no, so instead, we let the much harsher voice of life do it for us.

I'm going to close out this chapter with a few words from Neil Patel, an entrepreneur, a business consultant, and the author of the bestselling book *Hustle: The Power to Change Your Life With Money, Meaning, and Momentum*. In December 2016, Patel dropped a piece for *Forbes*—which I've read at least a dozen times—called "My Biggest Regret In Life: Going to College."

What a title. And if you think that's good, check out paragraph two of the article: "I wasted five years of my life going to college, and it's my biggest regret in life. For me, college was a waste of time, a waste of energy, a waste of money, and a waste of potential. If I hadn't have [sic] gone to college, I would be farther along in my entrepreneurial journey. I would have more businesses, more experiences, and more opportunity to make the world a better place."

I kind of want Neil to be my best friend.

The three primary issues he had with college were that he never learned critical thinking, the things he learned were useless (his words, not mine), and the way he learned was ineffective. Here are some of the article's highlights:

- ▶ "Seventy percent of the things my professors taught, I already knew. The other 30 percent was either wrong or outdated."

- ▶ "My professors probably thought I was a bit of an arrogant prick. In English class, I corrected my teacher's equation (not sure why she was doing math in the first place). She got mad at me, and threw me out of the classroom!"

- ▶ "College isn't a shortcut to success. In fact, it may be a roadblock to your success. College is not going to change you as a person. Nothing can do that for you. It's up to you to make the decisions that will take you to where you want to go."

▶ "If you want to be an entrepreneur, skip the school and go straight for execution. Hustle as hard as you can, and you're gonna nail it."

Neil Patel, you are my hero.

Sadly, Neil Patel isn't *everybody's* hero. When his article was reposted on *Medium.com*, the invective that was spewed in the comments section read like it came from a bunch of people who were stuck in a New York subway station during a heat wave:

▶ "My initial thought...spoiled whiner. Really? A college education is a privilege that many cannot afford—both here and around the world. I learned most of my critical thinking skills in college. In fact, I'd say that's where the vast majority were cultivated. I'm not saying it's right for everyone, but I hardly believe someone who wants to be an entrepreneur should automatically NOT go. There is no one formula to becoming an entrepreneur, just as there is no one formula to becoming accomplished in whatever your field of endeavor might be."

▶ "I liked the writing here but think your reasoning lends itself to a sort of 'I am better than you' tone. I do not believe I am better than you because I am going to college, whereas you clearly think you are better than people who go are going to college. Rather than making this a constructive analysis of the cost and benefits of college, you just alienated a lot of people for a choice they believe is best. Please don't impress your beliefs on others with a tone that says 'you are wrong' at every turn."

▶ "You clearly had none before you went, found every way you could to 'hustle' the system, set about hustling your fellow students to make it even easier, now you're trying to hustle your readers into clicking whatever bait it is you are selling…. oddly enough, the one thing I take from what and how you write, is that whatever it is your 'businesses' are about, I don't want any. No doubt it is some kind of multi-level setup where what you're selling folks is a shot at selling something to others for you to make a commission on."

▶ "If colleges weren't the blind, deaf and dumb employer-prospecting factories they are, top-heavy with bureaucracy and utterly lacking in personal autonomy among their assembly-line workers, with how obvious you made it that you were out to hustle yourself some passing grades by any means necessary, you should have been expelled from the place and maybe even prosecuted. But instead here you are, having a laugh on how easy the place was to hustle and suggesting that being conned was the marks' fault."

▶ "This is the worst advice I have heard for [sic] any entrepreneur. This is like telling the next big basketball dreamer to skip college and go straight to the NBA. Any smart and realistic [sic] knows that starting something from nothing is tremendously difficult task. Less than 5% of startups have an exit and of those even have less have a chance of making it big. What happens to those 95% failures that now need to go get a regular job? Guess what, everybody else has a college degree for those same jobs and your experience at a three people startup doesn't mean anything."

There are almost a hundred more diatribes, some pro-college, some anti-college, but all passionate. That's the way it should be. I'll listen to anybody's point of view, but unless there's some emotion behind it, I'll have trouble accepting it.

If you want to pursue higher education, you should be passionate. If you want to pursue a trade, you should be passionate. Don't be complacent. Don't follow the crowd. Don't go to college just to go to college. Don't skip college just to skip college. Have a plan. Have some conviction. Have a heart. Have some balls—balls like Neil Patel's.

5

As of this writing, I'm thirty-three years old, I'm recently married, and there is a child on the distant horizon. I've achieved a lot of the things I want to achieve, but my eyes are constantly directed upwards. I want to move up the next rung on the ladder. Now that I've gotten to the next station in personal life, I want to get to the *next* next station in my professional life.

And for me to get to my station, I need to get *you* to *your* next station.

I don't want people being mediocre. This country is too good—no, too *great*—for people to be mediocre. This is a country where you want to put it all on the line, where you want to take every risk, where you want to chase every single opportunity.

And that's what I want.

I want young Americans to not follow the crowd, to not comply with what is supposed to be done. I want them to do what is best for them. And in this book, I want to illuminate for them the options, the alternatives and the realities for their lives.

I'm hoping that my own college experience can help.

My parents were always very clear, from the outset, for as long as I can remember, that nothing came ahead of school. I remember even when I was at college, during my second year of university, my father came up to me—I was an adult at this point, remember—and said, "This council stuff? I just want you to know if I see in any way that it impedes what you're doing at the university, I will pull you out quicker than you can know."

That took me aback. A lot.

One of the big cultural differences between America and Australia, I've discovered, is that parents in Australia are like God. Down there, it's not like you turn eighteen and move out of the house to live on your own, whether or not you're attending college. The culture is like Europe in that respect, where you live with your parents until you're married. It always seemed to me that in Australia, most kids attended the college that's within driving distance or public transportation distance of their parents' house.

I lived only twenty minutes from the University of Sydney— and I was living at home—so when my Dad told me that he wasn't thrilled about how the council was impacting my life, I didn't have any kind of reaction other than, "Holy crap, this college thing is really important to my parents."

This is the conundrum that many potential American college attendees find themselves dealing with. They want to please their parents, so they'll go to school whether or not they're qualified, whether or not their family can afford it, or whether or not they even want to go in the first place. I may not have an extensive background in education, but man, can I speak with authority on parental pressure.

I suspect part of my father's insistence that I focus on education stems from the fact that he's a Greek immigrant, and like any immigrants coming to a new country, he wants each successive Adams generation to have an easier life. It was very much the prevailing judgment amongst previous generations that if you didn't earn a college degree, you'd end up laying bricks (not that there's anything wrong with that), and it was much better to work with your mind while wearing a suit as opposed to getting covered in mortar while standing in the scorching heat or the bitter cold.

I get that, and I respect that. But the thing is, whether you're in Australia, in the United States, or on Mars, if you're going to go to college and you really don't want to be there, what's the point? It can be even more pointless in Australia, where most degrees are very generic, thus do not have a specific profession at the end of it.

Yikes. That's depressing. So it's time for a couple of quick anecdotes.

Sanjay and I have been best friends since we were ten. As long as I've known him, he's wanted to follow in his father's footsteps and become a small business owner; be an entrepreneur. No exaggeration, at ten years of age, little Sanjay was, in his mind, a businessman-in-training. Good for him, right?

At some point during high school, I distinctly remember Sanjay telling me that he was going to go to college because he didn't ever want anyone assuming he was dumb, or trying to take advantage of him. But he knew that he wouldn't be going to school *for himself*. He'd be doing it *for everybody else*. (I think we all know what Neil Patel would say about that.)

So Sanjay went to school and ended up starting his own business, and making a good living for himself. Now there's no way to quantify whether or not college helped or hindered his success, but knowing him, I suspect he'd have been just fine had he gone straight into business from high school. See, Sanjay knew what he wanted, and what he wanted didn't require a degree. If there's one thing you take away from this book, I'd like it to be that. (That said, I'd also like you to have some takeaway from the trade school section near the end, because it took me *forever* to research that thing.)

Another anecdote. My friend Alan's father was the Attorney General of a state in Australia. (For those of you unfamiliar with the intricacies of Australian geography—which, I suspect, is all of you non-Australians—a "state" in Australia is like any of the fifty United States.) Alan's father was a pretty powerful guy.

Alan, however, didn't follow in dad's footsteps, which, as noted, is kind of a big deal Down Under. No law school for him—for that matter, no college for him.

Alan was a plumber.

Alan was a plumber who owned his own plumbing company.

Alan was a plumber who had thirteen employees.

Alan was a plumber who had a fleet of ten trucks.

Alan was a plumber who had a wife and three sons.

Alan was a plumber who made one hundred thousand American dollars a year. So, in anyone's language, Alan was a successful plumber.

Naturally, my father—a man who, if you'll recall, wanted to be a plumber himself—loves Alan.

All that said, when Alan started his business, he had a huge advantage over a lot of the local plumbers: *his father was the bloody Attorney General*. And the advantage comes from the fact that the bloody Attorney General has a good name and a ton of connections.

See, when you're a political family, you tend to have a lot of networks. If one of the people in your network is looking to get a broken pipe fixed, he'll say, "Get Alan. His father is the bloody Attorney General." (This brings up a minor, but still interesting point. If you're on the fence about college, but you or your family has a connection that can help you out with your professional life, you might well get more out of the connection than the university. Just a thought.)

But this story has a twist. One day earlier this year, seemingly out of nowhere, Alan threw in the plumbing towel, sold his business, and became, of all things, a lobbyist. He never told me this, but I suspect it had to do with the fact that all of his friends were guys like me, educated professionals who lived in the city. I think it bothered him that everyone in his circle had gone to university and now wore a suit and tie. I guess that he wondered, "How did the son of the Attorney General become a plumber?"

I've yet to hear how the lobbying is treating him. But I know for certain that as a plumber, he was happy, he was wealthy, he was fulfilled, and he was passionate.

Ah, passion.

Whatever choice you make—whether you choose to pursue higher education, or the fine arts, or underwater welding (yes, that's a thing, as you'll see later)—that choice should be guided, in large part, by passion.

Passion, to me, sorts out the men from the boys. I respect *anybody* who has passion for *anything*. Even if I disagree with them, if they are passionate about it, that indicates they have the courage of their convictions, that they're not plastic; that there's something human about them.

Because Passion is a very human thing. If you have passion, you're not a cold person, the kind of person who would enslave themselves in order to make it from one day to the next. We all know that life is a constant challenge, and your life can get thrown into turmoil in the blink of an eye, and it's a roller coaster ride full of really high highs and really low lows, but to get through that, and to persevere, and to persist, and to keep on against all odds, and to be happy and fulfilled even in the face of all adversity—that takes passion.

Passion is the root of all success.

6

Before I sat down to write this book, I Skyped my Dad and asked him, "How did you know I was college material?"

He looked at me with disdain, like it was the dumbest question he'd ever heard, and said, "C'mon mate. Don't be stupid. You were four, and I could tell."

I said, "Dad, how'd you know when I was four?"

And he said, "Nick, you just know. You can tell."

Ah, college material. That's a question that needs to be asked by a parent of a potentially college-bound kid, or by the kid him- or herself: How can you tell if the ability to succeed in school is in their DNA?

The answer is simple: you can't.

I could read or write a million books on this topic, and I'd still never know who or what college material is. But I can (sort of) tell you how my family and I knew I was college material, and hopefully that can help you decide whether or not to take the leap into higher education, a trade school, or the job force. Spoiler alert: I firmly believe that if it's clear that the student-in-question isn't college material, they should choose one of the two latter options. That, to me, is a no-brainer.

During that Skype call, my father related the story of a parent-teacher interview he had when I was in elementary school. The teacher told him that I was in the bottom-third of the class, and while he wouldn't tell me exactly what he said to the teacher, he did note, "That teacher was the biggest dickhead I'd ever come across. She had no idea. She was a complete idiot with no clue. Even at that age, you were switched on and cluey. You were college material, Nick. It was obvious to me. And I was right." ("Switched on" and "cluey" are Australian for, basically, "alert" and "aware.")

You'll likely get a sense as to whether you or your child is college material by the time their sophomore year in high school rolls around. At that point, you'll know whether they're adept at any specific subject—or, for that matter, whether or not they enjoy any specific subject. If they excel across the board, college might make sense. But if they're struggling with academics, while at the same time doing some fantastic work in, say, the wood shop or music class, it might be time to start exploring an alternative route.

Of course, as demonstrated by my father's reaction to that infamous parent/teacher conference, some of it is gut instinct. Let's say a child is earning straight As, but comes home from school each and every day looking and sounding miserable. They might give lip service to pursuing a college degree, but if your eyes and your heart are telling you, "This kid is hating their life," you should, at the very least, sit them down for a conversation—an honest conversation. A potentially life-changing—and life-improving—conversation.

> ▸ You need to tell the child your expectations. But you also have to tell the child that your expectations aren't

the be all and end all. In some cases, the parents' wishes shouldn't even factor into the decision.

▸ You need to ask your child if they're happy with their current school situation. Maybe they'll give you an honest answer, and maybe they won't—teenagers aren't always open with their feelings, as we're all well aware— but you have to give them the opportunity to be heard. Encourage them to dig deep and tell the truth without fear of reprisal. Part of the reason kids go to college when they don't want to, don't need to, or aren't ready is because they don't bother telling anybody about their lack of interest.

▸ You need to embrace and encourage open dialogue. Create a safe space where everybody can voice opinions, thoughts, and dreams.

▸ Most importantly, you need to go into this crucial conversation with an open mind. It's possible that your child is earning lousy grades, but nonetheless has a burning desire to become a better student and become educated at a higher level. Just because *you* might not feel they're college material doesn't mean they're *not* college material. It works both ways.

Once it was determined that I *was* college material, I went to the same university that my father went to because that's what I wanted to do. Being at University of Sydney was important to me. It made me part of my father's legacy.

If I wasn't college material, knowing what I know now, I'd have wanted my father to sit me down and say, "Look, Nick, you're great at this, and you're great at that, but I don't know that college is going to be the best thing for you because we have to be realistic as well. Life is all about choices. You don't want to have a hard life, and one of the ways to not have a hard life is to make good, logical, sound decisions. And besides, I spoke with your geography teacher, and he told me that you're about in the middle of the class, plus I spoke with your science teacher, and she said you're in the bottom third of her class, plus I spoke to your English teacher, and he said that on your last exam, you scored 52%. I think you're going to struggle at college, and why would you go and struggle at college when you can find a trade that suits you? Then while all of your friends are off at college, you can be earning and saving up money, and you'll be able to buy a home before anybody of them."

Which brings up the point that the teachers should have a say in the matter. The problem there is most teachers are afraid to speak up.

I understand that. Look at my father: when he started telling kids to consider alternative post-high school options, the administration was less than pleased. And I get that. If 50 percent of the students at a certain high school skip college, the principal would feel like they lost the battle, as would the superintendent—which could lose somebody their raise and/or their job.

I can say that with authority because—and here's something you won't believe, having read this far—*I can teach*. I have a post-graduate degree in teaching, and I'm qualified to teach both English and German.

Betcha didn't see that one coming.

One day during a tutorial while I was studying for my teaching degree, I piped up, "Look, too many people are going to college and they shouldn't be going." (Even then, I wasn't shy about my thoughts on this topic.)

The entire room—thirty people and one teacher—went silent. The glares could have burnt holes through steel. It was like I shot somebody's Mom.

And then after about a minute of dead quiet, all hell broke loose. Everybody went nuts. One cacophony of voices drowned out the other cacophony of voices.

After things calmed down somewhat, this girl got up and, almost tearful, delivered an impassioned story about her brother who was absolutely useless at high school, who couldn't write his name on a piece of paper and then miraculously, at the age of twenty-eight, went back to university, and now, at thirty-four, he went back to get his PhD, and that was great because certain people have an intellect that doesn't mature until later in life. It was both a heartfelt and a vitriolic speech, and the class applauded when she was done.

She capped it off by saying, "Nick Adams, you're an asshole." (Some people who are reading this right now might think that should be the title of this book: *Nick Adams, You're an Asshole* by Nick Adams. That has bestseller written all over it. It's worth noting that the teacher egged on the student, because she also thought I was an asshole.)

Now don't get me wrong: I'm not saying that all teachers are all about numbers, that they want their students in college because it reflects well on their teaching abilities. There are plenty of idealistic educators who think they can turn a mutt into a show dog, that they can take a troubled, lackadaisical kid and, through the sheer force of will, make them into a brilliant student.

But that won't work unless the kid *wants* to be made into a brilliant student. They have to have the desire and the capacity. You can't force someone to be something they're not, which is why you shouldn't force someone to go to college. There has to be some kind of realism across the board: realistic parents, realistic children, and realistic teachers, as well as a realistic society.

So I suppose now is as good a time as any to talk about Millennials.

7

There's a grain of truth in most stereotypes, because without truth, a stereotype wouldn't be a stereotype.

In a December 2017 issue of *Forbes*, Nick Candito, co-founder and CEO of the consulting company Progressly, said, "While there are exceptions, generally speaking, Millennials have less patience and fewer skills than people of earlier generations. They're more finicky, entitled, and restless. They're also less loyal to corporations, and usually take full advantage of happy hours, vacation time, and other perks."

It should be noted that Candito is, himself, a Millennial. *That*, my friends, is some serious self-awareness.

And then there's *The Guardian*'s Aisha Gani, who, in March 2016, listed her five favorite millennial stereotypes:

- ▶ Millennials set the bar too high because of a sense of entitlement.
- ▶ Millennials are lazy.
- ▶ Millennials work to live rather than live to work.
- ▶ Millennials are compulsive job-hoppers.
- ▶ Millennials have little time for experienced colleagues.

Whether or not you agree with these stereotypes, they're in the ozone, which might explain why there are so many unemployed Millennials...*who have college degrees.*

In 2016, *Newsweek* tracked down Anthony Carnevale, director and research professor for Georgetown University's Center on Education and the Workforce, who told them that Millennials with degrees make up about 40 percent of the unemployed in the United States. Now I wasn't a math major or anything, but if four out of ten twenty-somethings toting a college degree are looking for work, well, that ain't good.

Carnevale then went on to note that by 2020, Millennials will be an estimated 46 percent of all U.S. workers, adding, "Millennials are going to dominate the numbers, employment, and unemployment from here on out."

Which begs the question, if there's a four in ten chance you're going to be unemployed *with* a college degree, might it make sense to not bother getting said college degree? From a financial perspective, the answer is a resounding, *Bloody hell yes.*

In June 2018, *Forbes* reported that there are forty-four million American student borrowers who collectively owe 1.5 trillion dollars in student loan debt. They also noted that the average student in the class of 2016 left school with 37,172 dollars in student loan debt.

Almost forty grand; I promised myself I wouldn't curse in this book, but...*holy shit*! That sounds bad, but it sounds even worse when you break down the numbers.

As of August 2018, *SmartAsset.com* tells us that the average salary for a Millennial—a demographic they say falls between eighteen and thirty-four years of age—is currently 35,592 dollars a year. That's not enough to survive on in a major city like

New York, Chicago, Los Angeles, Boston, or San Francisco, so let's say that the Millennial graduate decides to live in a city with affordable rents like Cleveland, Ohio, where *RentCafe.com* tells us that, as of August 2018, you can get a decent studio apartment for 684 dollars a month. *SmartAsset.com* tells us that after Ohio taxes, your yearly take-home pay will be 28,728 dollars, 8,202 dollars of which will go towards rent, leaving you with 1,723 dollars a month to play with. Factoring in your food, phone, and electricity bills, that doesn't leave you with enough money for cable television and a few movie nights, let alone a student loan payment. If nothing else, skipping college eliminates that particular headache.

SmartAsset.com also tells us that, admittedly, the average 2018 salary for a college graduate is 59,124 dollars, but in terms of earning, they're four years behind our straight-out-of-high-school wunderkind. Not only are they saddled with the aforementioned loan, but they missed out on the four years of earnings where, on average, their non-college counterparts raked in 142,368 dollars.

And another thing: that 35,592 dollars average salary includes retail workers who, as of this writing, according to the Bureau of Labor Statistics, earn 23,110 dollars per year. And 35,592 dollars average salary includes restaurant servers who, as of this writing, according to *GlassDoor.com*, earn 14,702 dollars per year.

If you have the wherewithal to read this book, chances are you or your loved one has higher professional aspirations. Not to disparage the service industry, but I'm all about entrepreneurship. And as my hero Neil Patel made clear several chapters back, a college degree won't necessarily make you a successful entrepreneur.

There's no guarantee that if you make the leap from high school into the workforce, you'll succeed, but on the other hand, there's also no guarantee that if you make the leap from high school to college, you'll succeed. That being the case, if you're a Millennial high school student, or the parent of a millennial high school student, look at where the Millennials are at right now, and ask yourself, is that where you want yourself or your loved one to be in four years?

Here's my theory: for the pursuit of happiness, it helps to have your pocket full of money. For that to happen, you need to make yourself *valuable* to society, and when you do that, you'll never be short of money. That can only happen when you are good at—or the best at—what you do, whether you are a doctor or a toilet cleaner.

Perhaps this pragmatic approach may be more insightful and lead to better outcomes than following the advice of family members or succumbing to the pressures of the prevailing cultural norm.

Let me also say, the skills learned in a trade school are specialized to earn you an income. They are not available at most universities where critical thinking is considered central to a university education. The difference is this: critical thinking at university certainly *assists* in putting money in your pocket, but in no way is it comparable to a specialized skill taught at a trade school, which should virtually *guarantee* putting money in your pocket!

From what I've seen in my travels throughout America— and, for that matter in other parts of the world—it seems to me that there is a shortage of well-trained technicians and trades-men. And I feel most young people would be better served learning a definitive skill set rather than a theoretically-based tertiary education.

If you aren't college material, you should take this to heart.

But guess what?

If you *are* college material—same deal.

Same deal.

8

Thus far, I've discussed kids who maybe shouldn't go to college, and parents who should consider not sending their kids to college. One group I've left out is the parents who want their child to get next level schooling, but the kid wants to take a pass.

Let's say your child graduated as valedictorian of their high school with a 4.0 grade point average. Let's say they were accepted early to an Ivy League school. Let's say the Ivy League school offered the child some scholarship money.

Now let's say that the week after high school graduation—the week after the brilliant valedictory speech, the week after an official at the aforementioned Ivy League school called the house just to check in—the child tells the parent, "Screw Harvard, I want to act."

That would be a tough one to swallow, even for me.

On the surface, our valedictorian is the dictionary definition of college material: great grades, great work ethic; great prospects. Taking a pass on Harvard makes absolutely zero sense. This kid has the world in the palm of his hand.

Thing is, the kid obviously doesn't want the world in the palm of his hand. He wants to be an artist.

This issue could have been handled earlier on had the child better communicated his acting dreams to the parent or had the parent better listened to the child if or when they were communicating their acting dreams. (Yes, people, it's a two-way street.) Had they managed to get on the same page, the child could have transferred to an arts high school, or applied to an arts college, or tried to find an actor or actors with whom to apprentice.

At the risk of sounding hypocritical, if I were in that situation—if my brilliant, accomplished high school student told me he or she wanted to pursue film, television, or stage—I wouldn't be thrilled. *Glassdoor.com* tells us that in 2018, actors earned an average of 35,310 dollars a year, and as much as I want my valedictorian to shoot for their artistic goals, I want him or her to pull down more than that salary.

However, if my valedictorian told me, "While I pursue my acting, I'm going to school to learn to be a physical therapy aid," I'd be thrilled, because *Glassdoor.com* also tells us that physical therapy aides average 57,430 dollars.

Listen, my heart goes out to any parent whose child is insanely talented and wants to go and do something that you know is not going to give any kind of financial security—read: the arts. It'll be a financial roller coaster, for a logical reason: without any kind of consistent infrastructure, writers, musicians, and actors can do all the brilliant work in the world, but they won't be able to earn a quality living until they're discovered, and if being discovered were easy, there'd be more successful artists out there.

I can speak from personal experience on this one. It took me a hell of a long time before I was able to get consistent work as a speaker and a writer. It involved going from convention to convention; it involved trying to find one connection after another; it involved researching the industry to death; and it involved constant hustle.

But if your artsy-fartsy child comes to you with a plan that includes an *alternate* plan, that demonstrates they're serious, they're tenacious, they're invested, and they're passionate. One of my high school friends was a saxophone player—a damn good one, as a matter of fact—and he told his parents that he was going to skip college to both play saxophone and work at a local record store.

They weren't thrilled. For that matter, they were livid. But after a handful of knock-down, drag-out arguments, my friend wore them down. He convinced them that he could and would succeed.

After a year, he was earning a nice salary gigging on weekends and working forty hours a week at the shop. After five years, in addition to taking on higher-profile, better-paying saxophone jobs, he was managing the record shop. The story has a brilliant ending: he now owns the shop and still plays shows around the city. He had a passion, he had a plan, he executed the plan, and he succeeded.

This is why you need to listen to your children, even when they're telling you things you never wanted to hear.

I can't sit here and tell you that these conversations will *ever* be easy. Honestly, I couldn't imagine having that discussion with my elders when I was eighteen, in part because it wouldn't have made a damn bit of difference. The prevailing attitude was, *Just go and get the certificate, just go and get the diploma, just go and get the qualification and once you've got the paper, you can go and do whatever you want to do, but have it.* Their idea was that the diploma-haver would always be secure. *Once you have the paper,* the thinking went, *you'll be untouchable. If you've got a degree, you'll always be able to go out and get a job and money.*

And that sentiment was unanimous. My parents felt that way, as did my relatives, as did my friends, as did my teachers, and (probably) as did the next-door neighbor. If I sauntered up to any of them and said, "Yeah, um, I'm kind of sort of maybe possibly thinking it might be a good idea to skip college and go right to work at...."

The conversation would have ended there. But that was then. That doesn't have to be the case today. For that matter, it *shouldn't* be the case. Because you can have the paper, but still be broke and miserable.

Right now, you might be saying, "Easy for you to say, Nick. You're not a parent yet." Okay, that's fair. But one thing I know for certain is that when I *do* become a parent, my number one priority will be to do everything within my power to make certain my kid is happy. And if they're happy, you should be happy...as long as they aren't robbing banks or hacking into the nation's power grid just for fun.

If my child is happy as a server at a diner, I'm happy.

If my child is happy being a bouncer at a nightclub, I'm happy.

If my child is happy apprenticing with an auto mechanic, I'm happy.

If my child is happy not going to college, I'm happy.

And your chances of happiness increase exponentially if you write your own ticket, regardless of how long it takes for the ticket to be cashed. It took me a long time to get paid for speaking events, and it took a long time to have a publisher publish one of my books, but man, it was worth the wait. There's no better feeling in the world than being a self-made man. If you succeed on your own terms—if it was you and your vision and your determination that made everything come to fruition—that's the best feeling in the world. You did not settle. You did not embrace mediocrity. You decided to lead the life that you wanted to lead, and there were no shackles, and there are no limitations.

Once you have that confidence, once you get that wind at your back, then you can really set sail. That's just the start.

9

Here's a thought: maybe college would take on a lesser role in young people's lives if high schools were better.

Okay, maybe *better* isn't the right word. Let's go with *different*. Or maybe *cooler*.

Better, different, or cooler high schools will lead to two things: students who are excited about furthering their education, and students who are fulfilled after graduation to the point that they're properly prepared for the real world *without* furthering their education. An entirely (well, mostly) positive high school experience will easily (well, relatively easily) distinguish those who will or won't soon thrive in either college or professional life.

One of the better/different/cooler alternative high schools in the country is New York City's City-As-School. A public school located in Greenwich Village (ah, the Village...I like it already), City-As-School is less about schooling and more about life preparation.

In 2015, *Business Insider's* Melia Robinson wrote, "In addition to its emphasis on real-world learning, City-As-School challenges the status quo in a number of ways. Students complete a portfolio of papers and projects instead of taking tests. There are no grades, no statewide Regents exams (minus the English assessment), and no class years. You graduate when you've completed your portfolio."

The school's origin story is one of altruism and a desire for change. Robinson continued,

> Founding principal Frederick J. Koury opened the school because he believed education shouldn't just take place inside the four walls of a classroom. As a teacher at his previous school, he took students on field trips all the time. His aspiration with City-As-School was to turn New York City's five boroughs into a playground for experiential learning. He established contacts throughout the city, armed students with bus and subway tokens, and sent them on their way.

City-As-School's website breaks it down succinctly and, in a way, inspirationally: "City-As-School (CAS) emphasizes **freedom**, **trust**, and **responsibility**." [Boldface in original.] The website continues: "It's a place where students learn by doing; doing in their internships, doing in their class work, and doing on their own as they prepare their portfolios for graduation. Started in 1972 with 15 students and the staff of four, CAS has grown to a student body of 685, and a staff of 86 dedicated teachers and administrators. Despite this growth the school has maintained the same core values it had at its founding: open communication (everyone in the school is on a first name basis), personal freedom (we don't issue hall passes, there are no metal detectors and no violence in our halls), and personal accountability (students are responsible for getting to their placements on their own and for making up any days they miss regardless of the reason)."

Better. Different. Cooler.

Then there's the Grand Rapids Public Museum School in Grand Rapids, Michigan. In 2018, *Noodle.com* wrote of the school,

> Newly opened in fall 2015, the Grand Rapids Public Museum School transforms a museum into a classroom, in the process bringing education into a new and dynamic space. With a mission 'to inspire passionate curiosity, nurture creative problem-solving, cultivate critical thinking, and instigate innovation,' the school offers students unparalleled opportunities to undertake problem-solving and exploration via hands-on activities. Students also gain valuable experience with the collections of the Grand Rapids Public Museum, where classes are held, and which serves as the site of their place-based education.

Yes, that's right, the school is in the museum, the ultimate in coolness.

Dale Robinson, the museum's CEO, told *RapidGrowth. com*, "There has been this long, strong connection to educational institutions at the museum's core. We had to look back to inform ourselves where to go. We saw a very rich tradition in education. Looking to move forward, we asked, 'Could there be a school here?'"

Noodle.com goes on to say,

> The Public Museum School and other institutions within the Grand Rapids Public School System are redefining what a classroom looks like. Museums, zoos, and other public centers are no longer relegated to field trips, but instead serve

as schools themselves. At these immersive sites, students gain immediate access to primary sources that serve as the bases for their academic and creative inquiries.

Principal Christopher Hanks is justifiably proud of his school's alternative approach to educating teenagers, telling *RapidGrowth.com*, "[Our] learning management system maintains a growth and competency model of learning that our students will be able to engage with dynamically. Rather than a simple accumulation of content, it reports on creative and critical skills, measuring that growth over time."

Hanks et al. must be doing something right. In 2016—just one year after opening its doors—the school earned a ten million dollar grant from the XQ Super School Project. On a more micro level, *GreatSchools.org*—the go-to outlet for those looking to get a gauge on the quality of their chosen school—gives the Grand Rapids Public Museum School an eight out of ten in terms of the category of student progress. Not bad for a school that's still wearing its metaphorical training pants.

Being that the school has been open for only three years as of this writing, we don't know the percentage of their student body that does or doesn't attend college. But considering the massive grant and the good reviews, one can assume that Grand Rapids Public Museum School attendees will leave with skill sets that will serve them well at university, or in the work force.

There are considerably more alternative high schools throughout the country than you might imagine—there are forty of them in Los Angeles, forty-one in Chicago, and fifty-three in New York. Even the tiny state of Rhode Island boasts nine, and the lightly-populated state of South Dakota has forty-four. So, if you, the parent, or you, the student, are both unhappy in the present and/or stressing about the future, find a nearby alternative high school—or even one that's not so nearby—set up an interview, and consider a new direction leading to a post-high-school decision that will be the rightest thing for everybody.

10

Time to tackle a touchy subject—as if this entire bloody book isn't touchy enough.

I'm not a fan of Bill Maher. He's a competent enough comedian, but I don't agree with about 95 percent of what he has to say. And I'm sure that if he heard me speak, he wouldn't agree with about 95 percent of what I have to say.

But I firmly believe that he should be able to say whatever he wants, wherever he wants. And one would believe that a college campus—theoretically a place where the goal is to open minds—is the ideal venue to spout off to your heart's content.

This is why I was offended when, in April of 2017, the University of California at Berkeley cancelled Maher's scheduled appearance after he told CNN's S.E. Cupp that the school was "a cradle for f****** babies."

Ironically enough, what set Maher off was the fact that that Berkeley officials cancelled an appearance from Maher's mortal frenemy, pundit Ann Coulter, out of concern that anti-Ann protesters might wreak havoc. That came just two months after Berkeley shut down an appearance by provocateur Milo

Yiannopoulos, an appearance that led to one hundred thousand dollars in damage perpetrated by protestors.

The Coulter cancellation even angered, of all people, uber-lefty former Democratic National Committee chairman Howard Dean, who tweeted, "I feel like this is the liberals' version of book burning, and it's got to stop."

Now Howard Dean and I aren't on the same side of *any* subject that often, but in this instance, we're buddies.

All of which is a roundabout way of saying that colleges should be a place that encourages open debate. When I went to college, I didn't want to be told what to do or how to think. I wanted to expand my horizons, to hear different viewpoints, to learn, to absorb. If a college administration doesn't want a speaker to speak their mind because they're afraid that the students will, in response, speak *their* minds, that's a problem not just on campus, but in the country.

I mean, if you can't argue politics in college, when can you?

These sorts of situations aren't limited to speeches at big campuses from big names. In March 2018, students at tiny Lewis & Clark College in Portland, Oregon attempted to physically block anti-feminist Christina Hoff Sommers from giving a lecture. The students chanted, "Which side are you on, friends? Which side are you on? No platform for fascists, no platform at all. We will fight for justice until Christina's gone." Yes, Hoff Sommers is a notorious figure—her thoughts on rape are particularly controversial—but she's not spewing invective and hate. (Note: I heartily believe in freedom of expression, but there's no place on or off campus for invective and hate.)

This trend has not gone unnoticed by the students. In a 2017 piece for the *Washington Examiner* titled, "I Go to UC Berkeley and I'm Seeing Free Speech Slip Away," Berkeley student Matt Keating wrote,

> College students need to step up and stop the pervasive suppression of free speech on college campuses. I enrolled at the University of California, Berkeley, because of the school's message that everyone's voice counts—that the home of the free speech movement still values intellectual discourse and divergent opinions. Unfortunately, political extremists are doubling down on efforts to shutter free speech at Berkeley and on other college campuses across the nation.

Keating then cited a *National Review* piece that reported ten recent instances of controversial (or even just semi-controversial) speakers being shouted down on college campuses. Keating then added,

> A recent survey by the *New York Times* finds that some Berkeley faculty members believe violence is 'acceptable' to shut down free speech when it is 'used against what is perceived as fascist intruders.' If used irresponsibly to describe those who disagree with you, I believe that buzzwords like 'fascist,' 'racist,' and 'alt-right' damage their power when calling out the true evils that they actually represent, and become ways of hiding from legitimate, beneficial discourse.

In the article, Keating never once mentions on which side of the aisle he sits, and it's difficult to glean from the context. He has a reasonable viewpoint, he cited facts, figures, and opinions from liberals and conservatives, he stated his case…and that's the way it should be on college campuses.

If I may go off on a quick tangent, this issue isn't limited to America. My native Australians are dealing with similar issues.

In July 2018, twenty-something Canadian Libertarian Lauren Southern was scheduled to give a talk at the Perth Convention Center. Members of a protest group called the "True Blue Crew" rushed the stage, disrupting the speech, and generally mucking up the whole night.

I don't agree with Southern's entire platform—she makes some good points, and she also makes some not so good points—but I admire her because, to some extent, she reminds me of me in terms of family dynamic.

The night before the speech, Southern told *news.com.au*, "I got kicked out of class a lot. Dad always told me to stand up for what I believe in, even if what [I believe] in isn't always popular."

Assuming she wasn't spewing hate and vitriol, Southern should have been allowed to speak in the classroom *and* at the Perth Convention Center, regardless of her position. The fact that she said what she had to say—and her father had her back—is beautiful.

This is a long, roundabout way of saying that the recent lack of acceptance on college campuses is yet another reason to reconsider an autopilot decision to continue with education after high school. One of the great aspects of college is that the new student is exposed to things they'd never seen or heard, be it a radical political view or an exotic piece of sushi. And if that's taken away—if discourse between students and students, between students and faculty, between students and administration, between students and guests is eliminated—what's the point? You may as well just stay home, watch cable news, and yell at the television.

That won't cost you fifteen thousand dollars a semester.

11

If you thought *that* chapter was touchy, wait until you get a load of *this* one. See, it's time to talk about liberal bias. The first question that needs to be asked is, "Is liberal bias a thing?" Are incoming college students more likely to be subjected to Democratic philosophy than Republican?

Absolutely.

There's something here. And it's *really* big.

I speak all around the country, pretty much all the time. At the conclusion of my presentations, I often have a parent or grandparent come up to me, very emotional, explaining how Jack or Jill had been this wonderfully traditional young person who went to church with the family, and was patriotic, and now when Jack or Jill return for Thanksgiving or Christmas, they accuse their family members of being racist, sexist, homophobic, and intolerant, often leading to Jack or Jill storming out early from the turkey dinner. And they now have all these strange ideas about gender, race and socialism, and are really sensitive to words that are used that they never reacted to before.

While colleges skew extremely to the left in terms of culture and politics all over the world—and typically influence students to that way of thinking—the issue is particularly pronounced in the United States.

Why?

Because in America, you tend to choose the college that is the furthest from where you live. On top of that, in American culture, you tend to be on your own once you turn eighteen… which happens to be when you begin college.

So, the college professors and student leaders are exploiting this uniquely American cultural loophole, a loophole that delivers the student to them, completely naked, so to speak. They have the student, in their entirety, at their disposal.

What do I mean by this?

I mean that in America, a student attending college is completely susceptible. In the majority of cases, the student is away from home, away from their family, and away from the influences they had previously. They're in a brand-new environment. More than that, a student begins college with great enthusiasm and a desire to explore, as well as fit in.

When they are exposed to these left-of-center ideas on campus, there often—very often—is no counterpoint. They aren't going back and having a discussion with their parents—with whom they might not even be in regular contact—or friends from their hometown about what they've heard. They're only ever talking about these things with people who believe the same thing.

From what I've seen, in cultures where the family unit is more close-knit and in constant communication, where the culture doesn't encourage parenting to end at eighteen, where students are usually still at home while going to college, there is a far higher probability that their children, despite going to colleges with the same political bent and force, will not be influenced anywhere nearly as much as they would be if they were in America.

The month I began writing this book (April 2018) a Brooklyn College professor by the name of Mitchell Langbert published a study titled, "Homogenous: The Political Affiliations of Liberal Arts College Faculty." In it, he tells us that,

"The political registration of full-time, PhD-holding in top-tier liberal arts colleges is overwhelming. Indeed, faculty affiliations at 39 percent of the colleges in my sample are Republican free—having zero Republicans. The political registration in most of the remaining 61 percent, with a few important exceptions, is slightly more than zero percent, but nevertheless absurdly skewed against Republican affiliation and in favor of Democratic affiliation. Thus, 78.2 percent of the academic departments in my sample have either zero Republicans, or so few as to make no difference."

Neal Gross, author of *Why Are Professors Liberal and Why Do Conservatives Care?* (Harvard Press, 2013) agrees. In a 2014 article for *Trusteeship* magazine, Gross wrote,

Professors do tend to be more liberal politically than other Americans. Although what it means to be liberal or conservative has changed over the years, social surveys dating back to the 1950s show that even then professors were generally more supportive of government intervention in the economy and civil-rights protections for racial minority groups and political dissidents. Today, surveys indicate that somewhere between 50 and 60 percent of American college and university faculty members are in the broadly liberal camp, as compared to about

20 percent of American adults overall. That makes the professoriate one of the most liberal of the professions.

Sure, a child should expect to hear dissenting viewpoints once they stroll onto campus, but they shouldn't expect to be brainwashed. In April 2014, ABC News writer Ryan Struyk wrote an article called, "What It's Like To Be A Conservative on a Liberal College Campus." In it, he told the story of Luka Ladan, a freshman at Vassar College. Luka's story began during the 2012 presidential election cycle, when Barack Obama was battling it out with Mitt Romney.

Ladan told Struyk, "I was in a class talking about Republicans—Mitt Romney and Jeb Bush. Whenever a name was mentioned, one kid would snicker and then five to seven would just laugh at the name." It got worse for Ladan after Obama won the election. "'[All the students] were just packed into a building. Everyone was cheering, ecstatic that they won,' he said. 'I remember sitting in my room because I voted for Romney.'"

Worst of all, Ladan was being peer-pressured into wondering whether he was right about, well, *everything*. "Sometimes I've questioned my beliefs because so many of my fellow students believe in something different," Ladan said. "Am I wrong with believing this? Is there something wrong with me? I remind myself that you should show resolve, but it's tough."

Gross believes the issue can be dealt with in a rational manner,

> While a conservative professoriate is unlikely any time soon, some things might reduce the hostility many professors feel toward the Republican Party. For starters, more GOP support for basic research in the natural sciences, the social sciences, and the humanities might help convince faculty members

that the party is not under the influence of anti-intellectuals. Colleges and universities should be in the business of giving students rigorous instruction in their fields of study, not social engineering, but the country would probably benefit if there were more settings on campus—for example, town-hall-like forums—where students from the left, right, and center could be encouraged to engage civilly with one another.

In February 2018, James D. Herbert, president of the University of New England, offered his own solution,

We must value ideological diversity in faculty hiring, just as we have valued diversity in ethnicity, gender, and sexual orientation. We can adopt strategies that have proven successful in promoting these other forms of diversity, such as: 1) making the issue an institutional priority; 2) ensuring ideologically diverse search committees; 3) training search committees to become aware of their own biases; and 4) actively targeting publications, organizations, conferences, etc., popular among conservatives.

Herbert went on to say,

We must also design academic programs and courses that reflect a greater range of ideological perspectives. This does not mean giving equal attention to all perspectives. There is no need to give more than passing reference to flat Earth proponents in geography courses, for example, since the data are clear on the question of the Earth's shape. But we must welcome honest and robust debate on controversial topics on which the evidence remains inconclusive.

Even the fine folks at, of all places, Harvard University find it to be a problem, and they also have some semblance of a solution. In May 2018, the Harvard *Crimson*'s Editorial Board dropped a piece called, "Expanding the Diversity Conversation," and in it, they wrote,

> Increasing ideological diversity—and making students who may disagree with mainstream campus ideas more welcome—should be worked toward beyond merely hiring intellectually diverse faculty, however. Initiatives to promote campus conversations in which beliefs are questioned should be encouraged, as should giving students the resources they need to feel comfortable but not unchallenged in their identities. By doing so, we expand the diversity conversation to make as many students feel as welcome as we can.

(The disclaimer at the end of the article is quite interesting: "This staff editorial solely represents the majority view of *The Crimson* Editorial Board. It is the product of discussions at regular Editorial Board meetings. In order to ensure the impartiality of our journalism, *Crimson* editors who choose to opine and vote at these meetings are not involved in the reporting of articles on similar topics." I know, I know, that doesn't add much to this particular discussion, but I nonetheless felt compelled to share.)

These are all logical, rational approaches: focus on the differing points of view, and marginalize the, shall we say, less convincing arguments. Nobody should complain about that plan. (Oh, yes, they will complain. But they shouldn't.)

Bias on and off campus might not be an entirely fixable problem, but that's okay. It shouldn't be entirely fixed—it should be *balanced*. Everybody is entitled to be heard, regardless of beliefs. Just because I lean right doesn't mean I feel the left shouldn't be allowed a platform on campus. But until the platforms are equal—until we can come together as a nation and the playing field is leveled—this bias is another reason that college might not be the right choice for you or your family.

12

It's all fine and good for me to go on about my friends like Sanjay and Alan, friends who made nice lives for themselves without having attended college. But you might be thinking, *Sanjay and Alan's lives are all fine and good, but what if I want more? How high can I climb without a college diploma?*

The answer is, pretty damn high. Here are some notable success stories:

Paul Allen: Business magnate
Net Worth: 20.7 billion dollars
The Scoop: Allen didn't need additional schooling to learn that he could get way more from his high school buddy Bill Gates than he could from Washington State University, a school where he could only handle two years.

Sophia Amoruso: Online entrepreneur
Net Worth: 280 million dollars
The Scoop: Amoruso is the poster child for kids who skipped college because they struggled in high school. Seems like she didn't need any formal education to find success with the clothing line, Nasty Gal.

Paul Thomas Anderson: Film director

Net Worth: 10 million dollars

The Scoop: The filmmaker dropped out of New York University film school after only two days. But that didn't hurt his directorial skills, as witnessed by his brilliant second film, *Boogie Nights*.

James Cameron: Film director

Net Worth: 700 million dollars

The Scoop: The *Titanic* director dropped out of both high school and college before becoming one of Hollywood's most financially successful directors.

Jim Carrey: Actor/comedian

Net Worth: 150 million dollars

The Scoop: The budding stand-up comic dropped out of high school so he could earn money to support his ailing mother.

Simon Cowell: Multimedia producer

Net Worth: 550 million dollars

The Scoop: The bullheaded Cowell left high school at sixteen and, through bloody hard work, built a multi-media empire.

Ellen Degeneres: Talk show host/comedienne

Net Worth: 400 million dollars

The Scoop: The comedian and talk show host managed one semester at the University of New Orleans. Her communications major didn't include any stand-up comedy classes, so it was likely a wise choice for her to move on.

Michael Dell: Computer innovator
Net Worth: 23.5 billion dollars
The Scoop: Dell's parents forced him to go to the University of Texas at Austin in hopes that he'd become a doctor. But once his computer repair business took off, it was bye-bye college, hello billions.

Larry Ellison: Internet trailblazer
Net Worth: 61.6 billion dollars
The Scoop: The computer magnate dropped out of college, not once, but twice, those schools being the University of Illinois and the University of Chicago. Apparently, Larry had no interest in being educated in the Land of Lincoln.

Arash Ferdowsi: Computer programmer
Net Worth: 1.1 billion dollars
The Scoop: Sometimes all you need is one good idea. Ferdowsi actually had two: Dropbox and dropping out of MIT.

Lady Gaga: Singer/songwriter/actress
Net Worth: 550 million dollars
The Scoop: This is a textbook demonstration of how an artist with supportive parents can succeed. When Gaga dropped out of college after one semester, her parents gave her their blessing, and the rest is pop music history.

David Geffen: Music industry maven
Net Worth: 8.2 billion dollars
The Scoop: Geffen took three shots at college—Santa Monica City College, Brooklyn College, and the University of Texas—before throwing in the towel and becoming arguably the music industry's most influential figure.

Tom Hanks: Actor/writer/director
Net Worth: 390 million dollars
The Scoop: Hanks left college for the same reason everybody does: to intern at the Great Lakes Theater Festival in Cleveland. Seems to have worked out.

LeBron James: Basketball player
Net Worth: 440 million dollars
The Scoop: The journeyman basketball player (after two stops in Cleveland, one in Miami, and one in Los Angeles, it's fair to call him a journeyman) was ready for the NBA in high school. Not after high school; *in* high school.

David Karp: Social media creator
Net Worth: 200 million dollars
The Scoop: Karp is an anomaly on this list in that he was home schooled. But home schooling gave him enough of the wherewithal he needed to create *Tumblr*.

Carl Linder: Farming leader
Net Worth: 1.7 billion dollars
The Scoop: The founder of United Dairy Farmers realized at age fourteen—the year he dropped out of high school—that he'd do just fine without a formal education.

John Mackey: Grocery store founder
Net Worth: 75 million dollars
The Scoop: The founder of Whole Foods decided that a religion and philosophy degree from the University of Texas wouldn't mean as much as opening his own grocery store. So that decision worked out pretty well.

Red McCombs: Radio magnate
Net Worth: 1.4 billion dollars
The Scoop: McCombs dropped out of school in order to sell cars. Then he dropped out of selling cars in order to create Clear Channel Radio.

Matt Mullenweg: Online communications expert
Net Worth: 40 million dollars
The Scoop: The eternally boyish creator of *WordPress* bailed on the University of Houston at the age of twenty, after getting huge offers from multiple tech companies.

David Neelman: Airline businessman
Net Worth: 1.6 billion dollars
The Scoop: When you have the kind of mind that can create Jet Blue, finishing up that final year at the University of Utah probably isn't necessary.

Jake Nickell: Clothing entrepreneur
Net Worth: 200 million dollars
The Scoop: If you've ever bought a t-shirt at *Threadless.com*, you'll understand why its co-founder and CEO didn't need any post-high school education.

Al Pacino: Actor
Net Worth: 165 million dollars
The Scoop: After performing badly at performing arts high school, Pacino dropped out and didn't embrace education until joining the Actors Studio. *Hoo-ah!*

Brad Pitt: Actor
Net Worth: 240 million dollars
The Scoop: The actor probably shouldn't be on the list because he dropped out of the University of Missouri mere weeks before graduation. But it's an interesting tidbit, thus his inclusion here.

Bob Procter: Motivational speaker
Net Worth: 20 million dollars
The Scoop: The inspiring figure didn't just skip college; he skipped high school, bailing after only two months.

Ashley Qualls: Online entrepreneur
Net Worth: 8 million dollars
The Scoop: At the age of fourteen, Qualls borrowed eight dollars from her mother so she could start her own business. That business became *WhateverLife.com.*

Rachael Ray: Chef/author/television personality
Net Worth: 60 million dollars
The Scoop: Talk about a hustling self-starter: Ray started a food empire without any formal culinary training or college schooling—an inspiration to all DIY-ers.

Kevin Rose: Computer programmer
Net Worth: 8 million dollars
The Scoop: Who needs a degree when you have the kind of brainpower and creativity that comes up with *Digg*, *evision3*, and *Pownce*? Not Rose, who now advises Google Ventures.

Russell Simmons: Record industry leader

Net Worth: 340 million dollars

The Scoop: After dropping out of the City College of New York, the so-called godfather of rap became one of the biggest music industry mavens of the 1990s.

Jack Taylor: Automobile businessman

Net Worth: 12.8 billion dollars

The Scoop: Taylor, who founded Enterprise Rent-A-Car, realized after taking business classes at Washington University in St. Louis that he'd be fine without a degree. And boy, was he right.

Ted Turner: Multimedia magnate

Net Worth: 2.2 billion dollars

The Scoop: Turner, a canny businessman, was fired before he could quit, getting kicked out of Brown University for (gasp) having a woman in his room.

Ty Warner: Toy innovator

Net Worth: 2.5 billion dollars

The Scoop: Here's a guy whose backup play was way better than the original plan of becoming a thespian. Turns out that inventing Beanie Babies was far more lucrative than acting.

Oprah Winfrey: Talk show host

Net Worth: 2.8 billion dollars

The Scoop: After receiving an offer from a local television station, Winfrey dropped out of Tennessee State University and never looked back.

Anna Wintour: Magazine editor
Net Worth: 35 million dollars
The Scoop: After attending the all-girls high school North London Collegiate, the magazine mogul decided that enough schooling was enough.

Mark Zuckerberg: Social media leader
Net Worth: 70 billion dollars
The Scoop: As was made clear in the movie *The Social Network*, the Facebook founder didn't bother finishing up at Harvard.

13

Meryl was college material and had been so since she was twelve (maybe even eleven). But that was little surprise, as her parents saw to it.

Born and raised just outside of Syracuse, New York, Meryl excelled in school from the get-go, racking up straight As from kindergarten through the eighth grade. Despite the fact that their bank accounts weren't exactly high, her parents enrolled her in the top private high school in the area, a school with a reputation for churning out Ivy League attendees.

Meryl kept up her streak of straight As for her entire high school tenure, even though she was far from being the perfect student. With her parents' permission, she took her fair share of mental health days, as many as three a month. "I used to complain about burning out, which was absurd," Meryl explained, "because I could get my work done without expending that much energy. But my parents were cool and concerned about me being happy and healthy, so if I wanted a day off, they let me have a day off."

Even when she was at school, she skipped class on a regular basis, but she wasn't alone. "There was a lot of pressure on us to get good grades, so a lot of us took a period off here and there…and yes, there were certain substances that might have been inhaled." But the substances and the time away from class didn't hurt her GPA. "I was lucky in that I was able to earn high marks without banging my head against the wall. But most of my classmates had to work their butts off. They were the ones who were burning out. Me, I spent a lot of time hanging out in the drama department." A clear sign that Meryl wasn't destined to be a captain of industry was that her passion lay in performing and directing. "I was obsessive. I read every book on acting that I could find, I watched every episode of *Inside the Actors Studio*, I was in every play, and I even adapted and directed a stage version of [the John Hughes movie] *The Breakfast Club*. It wasn't exactly Shakespeare, but it was fun. And I wanted to do more." Unfortunately, her parents weren't on board. "Not to disparage them, but my mother and father didn't exactly support my acting endeavors. Sure, they came to all the plays and clapped when they should clap, but whenever I discussed studying acting in college, they'd quietly freak out. They didn't get angry, per se, but they definitely put out the vibe that acting wouldn't work for them. It was Ivy League or bust."

With her 4.0 GPA and her solid list of electives, Meryl was accepted by the only two schools to which she applied: Yale and Stanford. "Stanford was my top choice, by far. I'd never been to California, and I was tired of Syracuse winters, so I was eager to go west." Her parents, however, wanted her to stay closer to home. "They were footing a good chunk of the bill, and Yale offered me some scholarship money, so I kind of had no choice."

It should be noted that even though her parents paid a goodly chunk of her tuition—and she also got some financial aid on top of the scholarship—Meryl had to work for all four years at Yale in order to make tuition. "I was a part-time server during the school year and a full-time server during the summer. It was exhausting." Nonetheless, she maintained a 3.7 GPA through her first three years in New Haven.

By the end of her junior year, she needed a break. "I was fried, so I spoke to a counselor, who suggested I take a year abroad. I was all about that, but my parents were not into it at all. I generally didn't push back against them—I was the prototypical good kid—but I fought them on this one. Even though I hadn't been acting all that much, I still held out hopes of doing something in the entertainment industry, so after an absurd number of phone calls, I convinced a Yale alumnus to help me out. He landed me a job at a talent agent in London, so off I went.

On her first day in London, Meryl had a serendipitous experience that altered her life forever. "The people at the talent agency found me an apartment, which was more like a dorm: Tiny rooms, gray walls, horrible furniture, exactly what I was trying to get away from. Still, I was in England, so it was all good. After I dropped my luggage in the room, I wandered around the hallways, and a few doors down from mine, there were a couple of American girls chatting in their room with the door open. I poked my head in and introduced myself. Long story short, the two of them are currently my nearest and dearest friends. One of them gave birth to twins five years ago, and I'm the kids' godmother. If I hadn't have stepped away from Yale, they wouldn't be in my life. I'm forever grateful for that, as you can imagine.

The point being, sometimes the friends you make away from college are the friends that stick. And sometimes the friends you make in college fall off the planet after graduation.

Meryl worked at the talent agency for her entire time across the pond, after which she had a revelation: "I hated the entertainment industry. It was cutthroat, about half of the actors I dealt with were insufferable egomaniacs, and the creatives—the directors and writers—were unbelievably neurotic. It had been manageable for that one year, but the thought of doing that long-term stressed me out beyond belief."

Despite her ambivalence, she went back to New Haven to finish out her college career. "Academically, I totally blew off senior year, but it was by far the best year of school. I partied like a madwoman, I had an honest-to-goodness boyfriend, and I went to check out all kinds of live music. The best part was that I shared an off-campus apartment with two other girls and a guy—a crappy apartment, granted, but an apartment nonetheless. And the best part of living in an apartment was that I got to cook on a regular basis.

This was a big deal, because cooking was—and always had been—one of Meryl's great passions. "This is such a cheesy *Food Network* thing to say, but for me, cooking was evocative. My grandmother, who was the most important person in my life, was a phenomenal cook, and we used to be in the kitchen together all the time. Those were some of the greatest family moments. Living in the dorms, I never got to cook, and this was like coming home."

Despite blowing off, as she put it, "a zillion classes," Meryl graduated from Yale with that 3.7 GPA. After suffering through job fairs galore, she realized that 3.7 didn't amount to much.

"The problem was that I didn't have a specialized degree. You could have the best grades from the best school, but in 2010, it seemed like it didn't mean a damn thing on the job market." Even then, an Ivy League education didn't guarantee *anything*.

After decompressing back in Syracuse for a few months, one of the friends she'd met in London convinced Meryl to relocate to New York City. "Moving to Brooklyn without a job was just about the stupidest thing I could've done. But nothing was going to happen in Syracuse, and my friend—who came from money—said she'd cover my portion of the rent until I got on my feet. My parents weren't thrilled, but I was a grown up, and there wasn't anything they could do."

Meryl landed a job as a server at a chic-ish Italian restaurant in Greenwich Village. "I guess you could call it casual high-end. It was a pricy menu, but customers could still wear shorts to the restaurant." She became quick friends with the head chef. "He was a young, relatively cool guy. He was married, but he was into me—but he never got all handsy like, apparently, Mario Batali—so it wasn't too hard to convince him to let me help out in the kitchen."

In this case, helping out in the kitchen meant helping out with the menu. "He'd let me come up with two or three specials a month, always on Fridays. I'd never formally written any recipes, but I'd always been pretty successful in putting together dishes at home, so that was super-fun." Meryl nailed it right off the bat. "My first dish was a risotto with black truffles and some other stuff I can't remember. Everybody likes truffles, so it was a no-brainer, but the fact that we sold out of it meant a lot. I was kind of hooked."

Meryl had never given much thought to becoming a chef. For that matter, she'd never given much thought about becoming *anything*. "I wasn't earning enough money at the restaurant, so one of my friends from Yale got me a job as an assistant for a sports agent. Admittedly, I wasn't the best employee, and was fired after three months. No argument. I deserved it."

The only thing that brought Meryl any professional happiness was writing those specials at the restaurant. "That was my one opportunity to be creative. I began spending way too much time coming up with these recipes. But it was still fun." The chef who had the crush on her suggested she do something with her cooking skill set. "He told me over and over again that I was wasting my talent, and that I should nurture my skill set. He suggested I check out a culinary school."

In today's foodie culture, when most people think of culinary school, they think of the Culinary Institute of America (CIA), a relatively chi-chi school that, as of this writing, has locations in New York, California, Texas, and Singapore. The fact that the CIA has a chi-chi reputation generally keeps people from realizing the obvious: *it's a trade school.*

Back in the early-2000s, CIA's tuition clocked in at fifteen thousand dollars per semester, money that Meryl didn't have, and money that her parents weren't willing to even loan her. "They weren't exactly thrilled that I had, as my dad put it, 'Pissed away my Ivy League education,' so they didn't want to give me anything for *more* education. I also think that their generation looked down on that sort of school. A university diploma meant something to them, but a culinary school diploma, not so much." So, Meryl paid a visit to the CIA's financial department, who set her up with some student loans. "I wasn't thrilled about taking on any debt, but this was what I wanted to do. So I went for it."

She wanted to do it so badly that she took on an absurd workload. "I took two programs, one in culinary arts and one in food business management. I figured that someday, I might want to open my own restaurant, and if I had a background in both cooking and business, that would give me a leg up."

There was another student who was on the same fast track, and the two of them bonded immediately. "We started plans for our catering company before we even graduated. Everybody told us that trying to get a small catering company going in New York City was stupid because there were a million of them run by people who were much more experienced than us."

It turns out that "everybody" was right. "We got it rolling right after we graduated CIA, and it went nowhere. In six months, we managed to get, I think, ten gigs, maybe twelve, each of which was a nightmare. Our food was fine, and the customers were happy, but we never made any significant money, and the logistics were absurd. We always had to scramble for proper kitchen and storage space. Neither of us had a car, so we either had to rent or borrow one, because hauling all the food and drink on the train or in an Uber was ridiculous. A serious, serious nightmare."

But something good came out of it—something *really* good. "On our last gig, one of the guests at the party loved our food. She hosted dinner parties once a month, and she asked me if I'd be willing to cook them. She offered me way more money than I'd ever been paid to cook, so I jumped on it."

The first dinner party was a smash hit. As was the second. And the third. And so on. "After, I think, the sixth party, she asked if I'd want to be her personal chef. I knew personal chef-ing was a thing, but I'd never even considered it. I figured the logical path to success in the food industry was culinary school, catering company, restaurant chef. Being a personal chef wasn't ever on my radar."

Meryl worked for her new employer for four years, cooking her and her family lunches and dinners each weekday. "They treated me well, made me feel like I was part of the family. For that matter, they invited me and my boyfriend to some of their family events. I love them, and to this day, they're still a major part of my life."

Despite the love, Meryl was getting bored. "The family had their favorite foods, and I had to make these dishes week after week. For some reason, they loved my meatloaf. Granted, it was a really good meatloaf—I used beef, bison, and pork—but cook-ing meatloaf each and every week, even if you're getting paid well to cook it, can burn anybody out."

So Meryl began hitting up the online job boards, looking for something that offered a challenge…and maybe even health insurance. "A corporate chef job was the goal. My sort-of dream was to become a chef at Google. I figured they'd pay well, there'd be stability, and I'd have some fun."

Google, unfortunately, wasn't looking for a cook, but a small private equity firm in Midtown Manhattan was. "I answered their *LinkedIn* ad, and two weeks later, they called. I had two great interviews, and then, silence." By the time the firm's human resources contacted Meryl, she'd all but forgotten about the potential job. "I had to interview with two more partners at the firm. It was frustrating, but I figured it would be worth it. I was right."

The week after the aforementioned interviews, Meryl was offered the job. The salary was in the low six figures, health insurance and three weeks' vacation included. "The only downside was that the president of the firm is a health nut and a fad dieter, so I have to work within the parameters of whatever diet he just discovered. But they're nice people, and having direct deposit is great, so I put up with it. Besides, it's better than cooking meatloaf."

After six months working at the firm, Meryl paid off her CIA loans and found her own apartment in Williamsburg, Brooklyn. As of this writing, she's still happy at the job—even though she's "kind of sick of cooking Paleo crap"—and she credits her later-life educational choice. "I don't want to dismiss Yale entirely, but truthfully, I haven't done anything with that education. I was a pretty smart girl going into college, so I can't credit them with giving me brains. But at CIA, I learned stuff that I couldn't have learned at Yale—or, for that matter, at *any* general education college. It prepared me for a legit professional life. I don't regret Yale, but if I had it to do over again, I'd have gone right to CIA."

Hindsight being 20/20, it's easy for Meryl to feel that way. Going into a trade school after years of her parents and her private school pressuring her into enrolling in a general college wouldn't have been an easy choice. When you're a teenager—even a smart one like Meryl—you're not necessarily equipped to make that decision. But in today's society—a society that often embraces those who have a unique skill set and an obvious expertise—that's a decision that needs to be on the table.

If you choose the right trade school, you might well end up like Meryl, succeeding in the job of your dreams.

14

And then there's Mike, who was most definitely *not* college material.

Mike's parents should've seen it coming early on. "I freely admit that I mentally blew off school. Like, we're talking from kindergarten."

A product of a public school system in Chicago, Mike is an undeniably bright man—but he gives no credit to said school system. "Listen, my teachers were perfectly cool. I had an English teacher in eighth grade who liked the way I wrote, so he'd give me all kinds of books to read that were probably inappropriate for somebody my age, like Tom Robbins, Philip Roth, and Kurt Vonnegut. I ate them up, and it gave me a lifelong love of reading. So something good came out of that."

Another "something good" was music. According to Mike, "I listened to a ton of records when I was a kid, and all kinds, everything from rock to jazz to soul. One good thing our school did was that once you hit fourth grade, they'd give you free private music lessons. In fourth grade, they brought this local orchestra in to play for us—I still remember this—and the music teacher told us to pick our favorite instrument from the orchestra. I liked the trumpet. The guy played it with a mute, and I thought that was pretty damn cool. So I started playing trumpet.

There was a downside to Mike's new brass instrument. "I sucked. The problem was that instead of teaching us cool songs, they had us work out of a lame exercise book. If they'd have let us hear some Miles Davis our Earth Wind and Fire and said, 'Here's what you can do if you practice hard,' then taught us a few of their songs, it might've stuck. As it was, I took three years of lessons, never practiced, and quit. So that was a waste."

But that wasn't the end of Mike's musical career; far from it. "Our local high school was enormous, like five thousand people, and it was easy to get lost. You had to figure out a place to land, or you'd be totally adrift. We know [sic] I was a horrible trumpet player, but I still dug music, so I joined what was, in effect, the AV club." (That's "AV" as in "audio/visual.") "It was pretty dull, but the guy who ran it also led the jazz bands. He knew I liked music, and there weren't enough piano players to go around, so he told me that if I wanted to try playing, they'd cover the price of the lessons for six months. If I liked it, cool. If not, no sweat—nothing ventured; nothing gained."

Turns out that Mike was a considerably better keyboard player than he was a brass man. "My private teacher was an older jazz musician. He'd been around forever, and he didn't like teaching what he called 'basic shit.' He did exactly what my trumpet teacher didn't do: he gave me context. It made a difference."

Mike had a natural talent for the piano, something he would have never discovered had he not found a mentor. "It sounds simple—so simple that it's kind of ridiculous nobody tells you this—but if you come across someone who can teach you something you love on a one-on-one basis, well, that's way more important than regular schooling." It's at this point that Mike's parents should have considered enrolling him into an arts high school. But like many mothers and fathers of generations past, they believed that a traditional education was the way to thrive in America.

If Mike's success with the private teacher wasn't enough to get it through his parents' respective heads that he wasn't a traditional young man, his performance at his summer band camp should've done the trick. "I'd only been playing for, what, eight months when I went to this jazz clinic in Wisconsin, but I was one of the best piano players there—and it's not like the rest of the guys were bad. After my group's recital performance, the guy who was running the camp got on stage and said, 'This young man has been playing for less than a year! How about that, people!' In those three weeks, I developed a more useful skill set than I did between kindergarten and freshman year in high school."

Things progressed rapidly for the budding keyboardist. "I started taking lessons from one of the best pianists in Chicago, who, to this day, I consider one of my dearest friends. He was also a great mentor, and he still teaches me new stuff." He also became the school jazz band's star. "I started composing and arranging songs on my own. Nobody taught me. I figured it out from listening to records, and reading books, and trying and failing, then trying again."

(A side note to all the teachers out there: granted, not everybody in the world, whether they're an artist, or a science buff, or an athlete, has the wherewithal and passion that Mike possesses. That said, if the desire and talent are there, it should be nurtured and encouraged. And telling somebody to figure it out for themselves—to study and practice their craft on their own—isn't a horrible thing.)

By the end of his junior year—just a year-and-a-half after he took up the piano—Mike was performing in some of Chicago's top jazz clubs. "I was playing with, I think, four different bands, all older guys. The funny thing was that since I was underage, we had to lie to the club owners about my age. They'd be like, 'How old is your piano player?' and the guys in my band would say, 'He's 29. He just has a baby face.' Nobody believed us, obviously, but there were paying customers at the club, so they had to do what they had to do. Fortunately, I never got busted."

Another reason it was fortunate that Mike never got busted is that he started earning himself a whole bunch of money. "I was playing high-end parties—you know, weddings, corporate events, that sort of thing—and those paid as much as five hundred dollars a pop. Between that and the club gigs, some weeks I'd take home one thousand dollars. There was one week during my senior year when I earned—and I still remember the exact figure—2,350 dollars. And I was saving up my bread. I wanted to be in New York City, because that's where a guy like me can make a living...kind of. That required seed money."

The problem was that Mike's parents, traditionalists that they were, wanted him to go to college. "Man, there were some loud-ass fights about that. They'd yell at me together, they'd yell at me separately. Sometimes I'd fight back and sometimes I'd just let them go until they burned themselves out. The thing was, their pro-college arguments were always lame. They assumed that I wouldn't make it playing music, and that I should have a fallback. And I get that, and I respect that—they're my parents, and they love me—but there was a certain lack of respect. Just because I was eighteen didn't mean I didn't know what I wanted to do with my life."

Another reason Mike wasn't thrilled about the concept of college: the choices. "My grades still sucked, and I wouldn't have been able to get into a school that had a good music program. Plus I probably wouldn't have gotten into a school close to a city that has a music scene where I could earn some money and gig with good players. It would've set me back years. And I would've walked out of there with some crappy general degree, which would've amounted to exactly nothing."

So Mike headed east. "I finally just told my parents that I was moving to New York, and that was it, period. They basically didn't speak to me until the day I left. At that point, they started being, you know, real parents again."

The story has a happy ending. Thanks to the connections he made performing in Chicago, and the talent that was brought to full bloom through practice, work, and mentorship, Mike integrated himself into the New York jazz scene relatively quickly. Today, he tours the world, records with some of the world's finest jazz musicians, and makes a decent living for himself—which, for a jazz musician in Manhattan, is kind of a big deal.

If he had it to do all over again, he probably would've made the exact same decisions…or maybe not. "There's one school in the country that would've probably been good for me: Berklee School of Music."

Located in Boston, Berklee is a hotbed of jazz talent. Some of the finest musicians of this generation—everybody from John

Mayer to Wynton Marsalis to Diana Krall—studied at what is, in effect, one of the country's most prestigious trade schools.

"I play with a lot of Berklee cats," Mike says, "and almost all of them loved it. I had enough balls to teach myself more or less everything I would've gotten out of Berklee, but I did miss out on meeting a whole bunch of interesting people. But neither me nor my parents thought about going in that direction. For them, it was college or bust, and for me, it was New York or bust. Berklee would've been a perfect middle ground. So if I ever have a kid, and they end up having some sort of musical talent, I'm sending them to an arts high school, and if they want to go further, it's off to Berklee, or Juilliard, or some school that focuses on music or the arts. I don't want to quash that."

But he has strong ideas about college's place in his—or his potential child's—life. "I don't want my kid to go through what I went through with my parents. It sucked, and it put a permanent damper on our relationship." (The damper was such that Mike asked I not use his real name here.) "I want to give my kids their own head. If they want to pursue music, cool. If they want to be a doctor or whatever, that's cool too. But if they want to skip college altogether, as long as they have some sort of plan, that's also totally cool. A weirdo educational path—or a non-educational path, I suppose—worked for me, and if Mike Jr. wants to follow my path, I'll tell him to go for it, and I'll support him every step of the way."

15

So, as you now see, trade schools circa the twenty-first century aren't the trade schools of days past. There are diverse venues to fit diverse personalities, they can help you realize your dreams—even if those dreams aren't your typical dreams—and they can lead to a quality life that's both sustainable and soul-pleasing.

That said, even today—even as I write this in 2018—trade schools have a stigma. They're often looked upon as a lesser option for those who can't enter or afford college. That, of course, is ridiculous, because there are so many different schooling options available, many of which can lead to a career that's potentially more lucrative, more stable, and more fulfilling than the kind of job you'd land with a general college degree.

Here's a for instance.

In 2018, ironworker and ironworking trainer Greg Christiansen told NPR's *All Things Considered* that, "[parents] are definitely harder to convince [about the viability of trade schools] because there is that stigma of the six-pack-totin' ironworker."

Kairie Pierce, apprenticeship and college director for the Washington State Labor Council of the AFL-CIO, echoed Christiansen, saying, "[Trade school] sort of has this connotation of being a dirty job. [Parents say,] 'It's hard work—I want something better for my son or daughter.'"

Pierce, of course, is right. Which makes me wonder, what the hell is wrong with hard work?

Stigma isn't the only issue that keeps kids from attending trade school. It's simply a lack of knowledge and understanding of what trade school is all about. A December 2017 report from the Washington State Auditor's office explained, "Students can shorten the path to a good job after graduating from high school by taking career and technical education (CTE) courses that align with courses offered at community and technical colleges or through apprenticeships. However, this performance audit found that many high school students are not given the information or courses necessary to take advantage of these options." (The dense report runs a whopping eighty pages—of single-spaced, tiny font—but, believe it or not, it's well worth a read, and can be found at http://www.sao.wa.gov.)

What follows are several dozen types of trade schools or vocations, some of which you'd expect to see on a list like this, but many of which might both surprise and excite you. Each entry features the minimum skill set you should have in your back pocket, some recent salary figures (which either come from *trade-schools.net*, the Bureau of Labor Statistics, *U.S. News & World Report*, *Salary.com*, *Payscale.com*, *Glassdoor.com*, *Learn.org*, *Sokanu.com*, or *Indeed.com*), and a hopefully helpful thought or two from yours truly.

If you choose to go the trade school route, here's some good news: you might not live in a city that has your choice of specialty education institution, but worry not—many of the below positions offer online training. There are a ton of helpful online resources that can help you find the online school for you, one of the best being *trade-schools.net*. Just search for the type of school that interests you, enter your zip code, and *voilà*, options galore.

Something I can say with confidence: one of the below trades will undoubtedly suit you or one of your loved ones.

ACCOUNTING

What you need: A bit of an economics background. Nothing big. Just something.

Typical salary: In 2017, an accountant could earn approximately 37.46 dollars an hour, which translates to 77,920 dollars a year. The top 10 percent earned 120,000 dollars.

Nick's take: Admittedly, accounting isn't the sexiest profession in the world, and it takes a special mindset to deal with numbers all day, but if you have that special mindset, it could lead to a lucrative professional life.

ADDICTION/SUBSTANCE ABUSE COUNSELING

What you need: Patience, compassion, and a certificate in substance abuse or addictions counseling.

Typical salary: In 2016, the median average wage was 42,150 dollars, and the top 10 percent earners took in 70,100 dollars.

Nick's take: This isn't a job for someone looking for a huge payday. But if you want to help others and make a decent living in the process, this is a great option.

ADMINISTRATIVE ASSISTANT

What you need: Become an expert with as much business software as possible. Microsoft Office for PC and Mac is essential.

Typical salary: In 2017, assistants were earning anywhere from thirty-five thousand dollars to sixty thousand dollars annually. A six-figure salary for a quality executive assistant in a major city is far from uncommon.

Nick's take: It might seem silly to say that being an A.A. could be fun, but if you're a people-person, and you're a nurturing type, this might be an enjoyable way to spend forty-plus hours a week.

AIRCRAFT MECHANICS

What you need: An Airframe & Powerplant (A&P) certificate from the Federal Aviation Administration.

Typical salary: In 2016, the median annual pay for aircraft mechanics and service technicians was 60,270 dollars, with the highest earners taking in 87,880 dollars. And yearly bonuses are commonplace.

Nick's take: Fixing airplanes is an undeniably cool job. After all, being a mechanic is cool, and this is like being a mechanic on steroids.

ALTERNATIVE MEDICINE

What you need: There are several certificates that will put you on the proper path, depending on what discipline you want to study, including certifications from the National Certification Board for Therapeutic Massage and Bodywork, the North American Board of Naturopathic Examiners, the Council for Homeopathic Certification, and the National Certification Commission for Acupuncture and Oriental Medicine.

Typical salary: Due to the individualistic nature of the professional—meaning you'll more likely than not be working for yourself—there's no such thing as a typical holistic medical practitioner's salary.

Nick's take: Many of us want to help heal the sick, but so few of us have what it takes to deal with medical school (i.e., the money). You won't necessarily cure all of your patients—that's the nature of the holistic beast—but you'll make plenty of people feel healthier, and if that's not a great endgame, I don't know what is.

ANESTHESIA TECHNICIAN

What you need: Make sure that your school of choice is recognized by the American Society of Anesthesia Technologists and Technicians.

Typical salary: The range in 2017 was a wide one, with 27,560 dollars being the low end and 72,390 dollars up top.

Nick's take: This, like all the healthcare vocations on this list, is a hugely important job, and if you're good at it, you'll work as long as you'd like.

ANIMATION

What you need: A strong computer background and a deep knowledge of popular culture.

Typical salary: As is the case with virtually every position in the entertainment industry, the range is all over the place. You might be doing some of your work on spec (meaning for no money in hopes that somebody will hire you), or you might end up earning seven-figures at Pixar.

Nick's take: There isn't a clear career path for an animator, but if you're passionate about cartoons, and you have an artistic bent, and you're patient and diligent, it could be worth rolling the dice on animation school.

APPLIANCE REPAIR

What you need: Not much, as you can apparently learn everything you need to know in a mere six weeks. I suppose a working knowledge of tools would be a good thing, though.

Typical salary: Newbies take in about twenty dollars an hour, while veterans run closer to thirty dollars, which gives you a yearly salary of somewhere between forty-one thousand dollars and sixty-two thousand dollars.

Nick's take: As is the case with virtually every household repair position, you will never be without work—and I can say that with authority, because as I write this, I'm waiting for a repairman to replace the pump on my washing machine.

ARCHITECTURE

What you need: Be solid on computer aided drafting (CAD) software, or don't bother.

Typical salary: In 2015, the median architect's salary came in at 76,100 dollars. But I personally know an architect who took in over a million bucks last year. And guess what: *he didn't go to college.*

Nick's take: This is definitely one of those professions where the sky is the limit, both literally and figuratively. (Skyscrapers, and all that.) If you have a great imagination and the ability and desire to market yourself, designing structures could lead to lifelong financial and personal fulfillment.

AUDIO PRODUCTION

What you need: A better-than-working knowledge of recording software, i.e., Pro Tools, Apple Logic Pro X, and Ableton.

Typical salary: In 2017, a sound engineer could earn anywhere from 68,180 to 125,230 dollars, while a music producer's salary ran the gamut from 82,310 to 189,870 dollars.

Nick's take: Unlike our friend Mike from the previous chapter, you might not have the requisite talent to make a living playing music. (No shame in that. It ain't easy.) But if you have an affinity for music and a good pair of ears, this could be a more stable, lucrative path.

AUTO BODY

What you need: Nothing is absolutely necessary, but an apprenticeship at your local body shop would certainly help. (As you'll see, apprenticeships are huge for potential trade school attendees.)

Typical salary: In 2017, a newcomer to the auto body world could pull in 41,970 dollars, while an experienced body man could make 70,670 dollars.

Nick's take: Think about how many times you've had to visit your local body shop. Then think about how much you've had to pay them. You get the point.

AUTOMOTIVE

What you need: As is the case with a body man, shoot for an apprenticeship.

Typical salary: In 2016, a mechanic could earn in the neighborhood of forty thousand dollars, while the top 10 percent took in approximately sixty thousand. But in an early-2018 report, the Department of Labor claimed the financial outlook for mechanics is "bright," so that number could amp up in the near future.

Nick's take: Remember what I said about an auto body man? Same thing applies here.

AVIATION

What you need: You can head into your aviation school with a love of airplanes, an open mind, and a current driver's license.

Typical salary: There are so many options to choose from (aviation and avionics maintenance, air traffic control and dispatching, piloting and in-flight services, airport and airline management services, weather science and aerospace engineering) that the money varies wildly. Suffice it to say that if you succeed somewhere in this industry, you'll be fine to the tune of six figures.

Nick's take: Talk about a stable position. People will *always* need to fly, so if you're good at your job, it can last you a lifetime.

BAKING AND PASTRY

What you need: Upper body strength and stamina. This isn't about making pretty cakes. This is about waking up at 4:00 AM and throwing together the best bread ever.

Typical salary: In 2015, an average baker's salary was 24,170 dollars.

Nick's take: I've met some bakers, and they're all about bread. Not money. Bread. This is a tough job, but if you're good, it could lead to a high-end restaurant job, or bakery ownership. Lots of dues paying, but if you're a bread person, it'll be worth it.

BARBER

What you need: Not much. Just don't run with scissors.

Typical salary: In 2017, an average barber's salary was 30,480 dollars, with the top 10 percent taking in 48,480 dollars.

Nick's take: Barbers don't just work at barbershops, my friends. There are opportunities at hotels, resorts, salons, and cruise ships. If you can cut, you won't be cutting at the mall, but rather on a luxury liner.

BEAUTY

What you need: Cosmetology school is no joke. You have to have a strong base of makeup savvy or else you'll be left in the dust.

Typical salary: As of 2017, a beautician's base salary was 24,850 dollars, but that number could be doubled with tips.

Nick's take: What with the increase of venues that offer in-house cosmetologists—i.e., department stores and chain makeup shops—this is a fast-growing industry. If you love makeup—and there are plenty of you who do—you'll have ample opportunity to earn a nice living while fulfilling a dream.

BREWING SCIENCE

What you need: A wide beer-drinking palate. You won't thrive here if you've only had Bud.

Typical salary: In 2017, craft brewers were earning between 24,447 dollars and 46,994 dollars.

Nick's take: This job—as well as the schooling—has *fun* written all over it. Note: I had a friend who brewed his own beer in his basement…*without any formal training*. His beer was horrible. Then he got training. And that stuff was *good*.

BRIDAL CONSULTATION

What you need: Wedding planners have to know how to make *everything* look just right, but no matter how good the school is, they can't teach you taste. So, before you dive in, make sure you develop a sense of style for people, places, and things.

Typical salary: In 2017, the salary range for wedding planners was relatively wide, with the bottom end taking in 48,290 dollars, and the top 10 percent earning 82,980 dollars.

Nick's take: The schooling is far more difficult and wide-ranging than one might expect—after all, you have to learn everything from menu planning to the ins and outs of marriage licenses—but there will always be weddings, and people will always spend too much on them, so it'll be worth it.

BUSINESS ADMINISTRATION

What you need: Have an idea of what arena of business interests you, and research it until your heart's content.

Typical salary: In 2017, business administrators without an MBA were pulling in an average of 54,019 dollars.

Nick's take: All businesses need administrators, period, so you'll likely never be out of work for long. Admittedly, not too many people are overly passionate about this job, but if you're all about a regular weekly paycheck and want to leave your job at the office, this is a logical choice.

BUSINESS MANAGEMENT

What you need: There are a number of different paths one can take here—account management, hospitality management, human resources management, sports management—so pick one or two and research, research, research.

Typical salary: In 2017, a business manager's salary ranged from 71,450 dollars to 145,620 dollars.

Nick's take: The schooling is tough and competitive, so if you weren't a great high school student, this might not be for you. But if you have a passion for the business world—and you're willing to work hard to develop some security in your professional life—you could be an ideal candidate.

CARDIOVASCULAR TECHNOLOGIST

What you need: A love of and a curiosity about the human body.

Typical salary: In 2017, a CVT could earn as much as 90,760 dollars, with a low end of 55,270 dollars.

Nick's take: With positions available at hospitals, cardiovascular clinics, doctor's offices, medical laboratories, and diagnostic imaging centers, there are plenty of venues to utilize your cardiovascular technologist certificate.

CARPENTRY

What you need: This isn't just about banging nails into wood. Have an idea of your chosen field before you enter school, as there are myriad choices. Also, an apprenticeship isn't necessary, but it'll sure help.

Typical salary: In 2017, carpenters could earn anywhere between 45,170 and 80,350 dollars.

Nick's take: Workplace safety…building codes…project management…construction. This is a wide-ranging, diverse industry that isn't going anywhere. So, if you have even the tiniest love and/or appreciation for building things, there are opportunities galore.

COMMERCIAL DRIVER'S LICENSE

What you need: Before you can become a truck driver, you need a regular driver's license and the ability to stay awake and alert overnight.

Typical salary: In 2017, the salary ranged from 19,610 dollars to sixty-four thousand dollars. The wide berth was due to the large number of jobs that run the gamut from local deliveryman to cross-country trucker.

Nick's take: For some, getting paid a decent weekly salary for driving is a dream job, so the six months of schooling is well worth it.

CHRISTIAN STUDIES

What you need: Knowledge and passion for religion is obviously required, but this is also about business, so be prepared.

Typical salary: In 2017, a community service manager could earn seventy thousand dollars while a fundraiser could take in 127,000 dollars.

Nick's take: If you have a Christian soul and a business head, you could be set for decades, both financially and spiritually.

CLOUD COMPUTING

What you need: Be good with computers. For that matter, you should be good with computers regardless of what trade school you attend. Even if you work with your hands, you need to know your way around both Macs and PCs.

Typical salary: This is a booming specialty, with a 2017 low-end salary of 86,430 dollars, topping out at 130,200 dollars.

Nick's take: As is the case with most computer specialties, there's plenty of job security or room for growth. Plus, if you're a self-starter—and you're willing to either get more schooling, or pick a colleague's brain, or study up on your own—the potential is limitless.

COMPUTER NUMERICAL CONTROL MACHINING

What you need: CNC is a fancy way of saying machinist (sort of), so an affinity for all that is mechanical is a must.

Typical salary: These days, the salaries are geographically based. For instance, in 2017, the mean salary in North Dakota was 45,590 dollars, while the number in Alaska was 66,230 dollars.

Nick's take: This may not be the most exciting gig, but if you live in the right area—and, of course, if you're good at what you do—the work should always be there.

COLLISION REPAIR

What you need: An apprenticeship at an auto body shop will give you a nice head start.

Typical salary: Since this is a specialized skill, the salary is higher than that of a typical auto mechanic, with a low end of 41,970 dollars and a high end of 70,670 dollars.

Nick's take: People get into car crashes. Always have. Always will. You'll never be lacking work.

COMMERCIAL DIVING

What you need: SCUBA certification, first aid and CPR certificates, and a diving medical exam from a qualified doctor.

Typical salary: The average salary in 2017 was 55,270 dollars, with the top 10 percent taking in 96,850 dollars.

Nick's take: One of the more exciting professions you can undertake without a college education, so if you're a thrill-seeker who likes the water and wants to make some good money, dive on in! (See what I did there?)

COMMERCIAL MAINTENANCE

What you need: A light background in electronics is helpful. A heavy background in electronics is even more helpful.

Typical salary: With a diversity of options (millwright, industrial machine mechanic, building maintenance technician), the salary is all over the place, starting at 40,280 dollars, and topping out at 80,090 dollars.

Nick's take: The Department of Labor estimates that the demand for millwrights, et cetera, will increase by 10 percent before 2026, so now is the time to get your foot in the door.

COMMUNICATION STUDIES

What you need: Words, words, words. If you have a way with language, you can excel at everything from interpretation to technical writing.

Typical salary: Considering the number of jobs available to somebody with a communications background, there's no such thing as a typical salary.

Nick's take: As somebody who enjoys writing—but doesn't have a background in writing—I can say that working with words is fulfilling on every level.

COMPUTER PROGRAMMING

What you need: A working knowledge of the most common computer programs, i.e., Java, HTML, and C++.

Typical salary: In 2017, an experienced general programmer could take in over one hundred twenty thousand dollars.

Nick's take: This is a win/win/win trade school option. No college degree necessary, computers aren't going anywhere, and good programmers are a hot commodity. So get a few computer-oriented *For Dummies* books and let the fun begin.

COMPUTER SCIENCE

What you need: The same thing you need in "computer programming." (see above) except a more wide-ranging, in-depth knowledge of all that is computing.

Typical salary: This is a more specialized discipline than computer programming—under this umbrella falls information security analyst, systems analyst, and network engineer—and the 2017 salary range reflects that, running the gamut from 74,110 dollars to 164,150 dollars.

Nick's take: Admittedly, you need to bring more to the table than you do to most of the trade schools on this list, but it's worth it, because it checks all the boxes: security, lucrativeness, challenge.

COMPUTER SECURITY

What you need: Knowledge of how to hack into a company's computer system. But you didn't hear that from me.

Typical salary: In 2017, the low-end salary for a security man was 99,260 dollars, topping out at 153,090 dollars.

Nick's take: I was kidding about the hacking…sort of. Often, it takes a previously nasty hacker to stop a currently nasty hacker. This is a high-demand position with not much in the way of competition.

COMPUTER TECHNICIAN

What you need: A solid computer background, but nothing too crazy.

Typical salary: In 2017, computer techs were pulling in a minimum of thirty-nine thousand dollars and a high end of sixty-five thousand dollars.

Nick's take: The mechanic of the millennium. As is the case with cars, computers always crash and somebody will always need to fix them. (Note: There are three computer techs in my neighborhood who *hung up a shingle* and run repair shops out of their house. Being that there's little overhead necessary, this skill set offers a terrific opportunity to start a business.)

COMPUTERS / INFORMATION TECHNOLOGY

What you need: Slightly more computer know-how than a technician, but slightly less than a programmer.

Typical salary: There are an insanely wide range of IT needs, thus there are an insanely wide range of salaries. For instance, in 2017, an Applications Support Technician pulled in 47,524 dollars, while a client/server operations manager earned 110,764 dollars.

Nick's take: The most difficult aspect of this position is the multitude of choices. Do your research before you choose your IT-oriented schooling. (Note: there are lots of online schools for this one.)

CONFERENCE MANAGEMENT

What you need: This is a fancy title for an event planner, so a feel for parties is a good starting place.

Typical salary: In 2017, the median salary for an event, convention, or meeting planner was 49,290 dollars, with the top 10 percent raking in 82,980 dollars.

Nick's take: Another job that can lead to starting your own business. For that matter, self-employed conference managers are often the preferred choice, as the less clutter involved in the planning, the better.

CONSTRUCTION AND BUILDING

What you need: No aspect of construction is easy—try being an HVAC (heating, ventilation, and air conditioning) tech—so passion for the craft is a must.

Typical salary: Lots of positions, thus lots of salaries. In 2017, it ranged from 33,430 to 62,600 dollars.

Nick's take: Don't take this job lightly. This is a tough gig—many variables, many disciplines—but if you're good, you'll be busy for decades.

CONSTRUCTION MANAGEMENT

What you need: Become a Certified Construction Manager (CCM), which can lead to a top salary.

Typical salary: This is a super-specialized position, and the 2017 salary reflects that, starting at one hundred one thousand dollars and climbing up to 159,560 dollars.

Nick's take: Before 2026, there could be as many as fifty thousand new construction management jobs, so now is the time to hop on board.

COSMETOLOGY (See page 95)

What you need: Makeup savvy. If you can't put it on yourself, you can't put it on anybody else.

Typical salary: In May 2017, newcomers and apprentices earned 24,260 dollars before tips and commission, with veterans taking in 49,050 dollars, also before tips and commission. And according to one of my makeup artist friends, the tips at weddings are quite generous.

Nick's take: I don't know much about makeup, or cutting hair, or being an esthetician, but I'm aware that there are a lot of them, and the ones I know seem pretty happy, and none of them are starving, so if you're passionate about beautification, the opportunities are there.

COSMETOLOGY INSTRUCTOR

What you need: Makeup savvy, as well as the patience to teach those who don't have makeup savvy.

Typical salary: In 2017, the base salary for a cosmetology teacher exceeded that of a cosmetologist, ranging from 38,889 to 56,600 dollars.

Nick's take: Teaching something about which you're passionate can lead to a truly fulfilling professional life. If you like beautification, but you are less enamored by the freelance life, this will be ideal.

CRIMINAL INVESTIGATION

What you need: Whether you want to be a private investigator or a forensic science tech, a healthy dose of curiosity is a must.

Typical salary: In 2017, crime scene investigators were taking in 61,220 dollars, while top detectives earned as much as 135,530 dollars.

Nick's take: This is difficult, often gruesome, often boring work, and that's reflected by the solid salary.

CRIMINAL JUSTICE

What you need: See "Criminal Investigation."

Typical salary: The wide range of jobs gives us a wide range of salaries, running the gamut in 2017 from 48,190 to 87,070 dollars.

Nick's take: This is a catchall umbrella for such diverse positions as policing the court system, to incarceration, to rehabilitation. Interesting, engaging, and often rewarding.

CULINARY

What you need: A good palate, the ability to follow recipes, and the ability to wake up really, really early and stay up really, really late.

Typical salary: In May 2017, the median salary for a chef was 45,950 dollars, topping out at 78,570 dollars.

Nick's take: Culinary school is a tough proposition—for that matter, being a chef is a tough proposition—so be prepared to work, and work hard. But if you're a true food lover, that won't be a problem.

DATABASE ADMINISTRATOR

What you need: A working knowledge of such database programs as MySQL.

Typical salary: In 2017, top earners in his field were taking in as much as 132,420 dollars, with a low end of 106,390 dollars.

Nick's take: While database administration isn't as exciting as programming, it's more lucrative, and easier to land a position. It's a terrific day job for creative types who are willing to do their fun computer stuff after hours.

DENTAL ASSISTANT

What you need: The ability to work well with others and not get squeamish in the face of bad teeth and/or bad breath.

Typical salary: The median salary in 2017 was 37,630 dollars, with the top earners taking in 53,130 dollars.

Nick's take: This is for those of you who like dentistry, but don't want to dive into somebody's mouth. It's about making the doctor's life safe and easy, not cleaning teeth.

DENTAL HYGIENIST

What you need: To get into a dental hygienist school, you have to pass an entrance exam as well as a dexterity exam. (And yes, a dexterity exam is a thing.)

Typical salary: The fact that quality dental hygienists are in demand is reflected in the 2017 salary, which ranged from 74,070 to 101,330 dollars.

Nick's take: This is almost like being a dentist without dealing with the cost of dental school. How cool is that?

DESIGN

What you need: If you don't have a good eye and a sharp sense of style, it's probably best to look elsewhere.

Typical salary: As you'll see momentarily, there's no such thing as a typical salary, because there's no such thing as a typical design position.

Nick's take: Here's where this schooling can take you: Graphic design, visual communication, visual arts, photography, advertising, architectural design, computer-aided drafting, interior design, industrial design, fashion design, floral design, media arts, animation, special effects, music production, music recording arts, video game design, or web design. Opportunities galore for creative types!

DIESEL MECHANIC

What you need: As is the case with most repair-heavy positions, an apprenticeship is essential.

Typical salary: In 2017, the median salary for a diesel mechanic was 46,360 dollars with a ceiling of 69,870 dollars.

Nick's take: The schooling in and of itself could be more than a little appealing to car buffs, with classes in everything from diagnostic equipment to engine rebuilding. And even when flying cars take over the world, you'll still always work.

DOG TRAINING

What you need: If you don't love animals, don't bother.

Typical salary: In 2017, the hourly rates for a dog trainer came in between 16.71 dollars and 26.92 dollars.

Nick's take: The money may not be mind-blowing, but if you're a dog fanatic who likes to make their own hours, dog training school could lead to a happy life.

DRAFTING

What you need: Familiarity with CAD, CADD, and AutoCAD software.

Typical salary: In 2017, this highly specialized profession offered salaries between 53,990 and 97,970 dollars.

Nick's take: This isn't just about drawing pictures of buildings, folks. You can also become an expert in mechanical drafting, civil drafting, electronics drafting, aeronautical drafting, and pipeline drafting—plenty of work available for the go-getter.

EARLY CHILDHOOD EDUCATION

What you need: Patience with the little ones.

Typical salary: This schooling gives you the skills to be everything from a babysitter to a childcare center director, which is reflected by the wide salary range in 2017 of between 17,490 and 85,240 dollars.

Nick's take: This one is all about the long game. You're not going to walk out of school and into a managerial position. You'll need to pay your dues in pre-school. But if you love children between the ages of one and five(and who doesn't?) it will be well worth it.

EDUCATION

What you need: If you like imparting wisdom and can deal with a rowdy child or two, you should be good to go.

Typical salary: Being that public school teachers need a bachelor degree, this kind of schooling is for those who want to be a teacher's assistant, which, in 2017, offered salaries ranging from 27,950 to 39,780 dollars.

Nick's take: Many private schools don't require their teachers to have a college degree, so studying hard and paying your dues could lead to a job that will earn you a nice living.

EKG TRAINING

What you need: A high school diploma or a GED are required. Some nurse's aide schooling is preferred.

Typical salary: In 2017, EKG techs earned between twenty to thirty thousand dollars.

Nick's take: This schooling will get you an entry-level position. If you can get certified in different areas of the healthcare world, your earning potential increases exponentially.

ELECTRICIAN

What you need: Hands-on apprenticeship training isn't required, but it's highly recommended.

Typical salary: In 2017, the average salary for all electrical fields was 54,110 dollars, topping out at 90,420 dollars.

Nick's take: This isn't just about changing light bulbs, my friends. There is lots to learn and lots to do, thus there will always be lots of opportunities.

ELECTROCARDIOGRAPHY

What you need: Learning how to operate a heart monitor in and of itself doesn't require any special skills, but a good bedside manner will help you go far.

Typical salary: Admittedly, this isn't a lucrative field—in 2017, the salary ranged from twenty to thirty thousand dollars, but it's one of those professions that could (or should) lead to something bigger and better.

Nick's take: This job can save a life. Maybe it doesn't offer big money, but it might give you the chance to fill your soul.

ENGINEERING

What you need: There aren't any hard and fast requirements to get into most engineering schools, but either a knowledge or a curiosity about how things work sure helps.

Typical salary: Being that you can become anything from an electronics engineer to a mechanical engineer to a civil engineer to a chemical engineer, the 2017 salaries are all over the place, ranging from 64,290 to 176,900 dollars.

Nick's take: Just because you didn't go to college doesn't mean you don't have the ability to think critically. Quality engineering minds are in demand, so if you have a critically-thinking brain, use it.

ENTREPRENEURSHIP

What you need: An idea (or five), an attitude, confidence, and an unshakeable desire to DIY.

Typical salary: Being that entrepreneurship runs the gamut from running a lemonade stand to launching a start-up that Google acquires for eight figures, there's no such thing as typical money.

Nick's take: This one is near and dear to my heart. One of the finest qualities of America is that you can dream big, and starting your own business is just about the best dream you can have and (hopefully) fulfill.

ENVIRONMENTAL STUDIES

What you need: A keen interest in saving the planet.

Typical salary: There are numerous green jobs available to the altruistic soul—we're talking everything from forestry, to sustainable agriculture, to green construction—which explains the 2017 salary range of 64,850 to 133,670 dollars.

Nick's take: Regardless of your take on climate change, you should get interested in this vocation because it's becoming increasingly prevalent, thus the work will be there.

EVENT MANAGEMENT

What you need: Planning events may seem simple. It isn't. Get a mentor.

Typical salary: In 2017, the numbers ran from 48,290 to 82,980 dollars.

Nick's take: This isn't just about weddings and bar mitzvahs, gang. You'll need to plan travel tours, and concerts, and fashion shows, and fundraisers. There will always be travel tours, and concerts, and fashion shows, and fundraisers, thus there will always be event planners.

FASHION DESIGN

What you need: There are dozens of fashion disciplines—design, conception, software, drafting; sketching—so devising a specific goal would be a wise idea.

Typical salary: In 2017, your garden-variety fashion designers took in between 65,170 and 130,050 dollars. The big name designers are multi-millionaires. Aim high.

Nick's take: This industry is considerably more than high-end dresses you see on the red carpet. Somebody has to design children's clothes, workout gear, and pajamas. Why not you?

FASHION MARKETING / MERCHANDISING

What you need: Being that you'll be trying to sell beautiful clothes in a creative manner, you have to have a good eye and a keen clothing aesthetic.

Typical salary: In 2017, you could take in as much as 111,950 dollars, with a low end of 58,180 dollars.

Nick's take: It's likely that you didn't grow up with a burning desire to market and merchandise fashion, but the opportunities are there, so get that desire burning.

FILM AND VIDEO PRODUCTION

What you need: In film school, you'll learn about theory, business, and technology, among other things, so you get both a direction and a keen knowledge of the industry.

Typical salary: This is one of those professions in which you can go a ton of different directions, as reflected by the 2017 salary range of 60,820 to 189,870 dollars.

Nick's take: Sure, most everybody can shoot competent video footage on an iPhone, but it takes a special someone to handle an honest-to-goodness camera. And you might be that special someone.

FINANCIAL PLANNING

What you need: If you're going to thrive at a financial planning school—and those schools are tough—you have to be a numbers freak.

Typical salary: If you're not a good financial planner, you won't work, period. But in 2016, if you knew what you were doing, you could rake in anywhere from 123,100 to 208,000 dollars.

Nick's take: This is a difficult, often unexciting training process—it's tough to get passionate about, for instance, tax code, estate insurance, financial computer software, or risk management—but it offers one of the heftiest average salaries for non-college graduates.

FITNESS AND NUTRITION

What you need: Easy: be healthy.

Typical salary: Personal trainers and nutritionists can work for themselves, or they can find a job at a small local company, or a public school. No typical salaries here.

Nick's take: Not only can you help others get themselves healthy—the job requires you to stay healthy. Getting paid to live longer isn't a bad thing.

FLIGHT TRAINING

What you need: A driver's license, as well as the ability to communicate, observe, and solve problems.

Typical salary: This is a tough, important job, which is reflected in the 2017 median salary of 137,330 dollars.

Nick's take: Traveling via airplane isn't exactly a bundle of laughs (when's the last time you actually had a good airport experience?), but it's a necessary evil, and it always will be, so a quality pilot will always be in demand.

FLORAL DESIGN

What you need: If you don't have a love of flowers and a good eye, it's probably best to look elsewhere.

Typical salary: This profession is no joke. In 2018, the salary ranged from 40,494 to 60,284 dollars.

Nick's take: This is a perfect example of a very specialized job for a very specialized non-college attendee. If you're a plant person, pursue this immediately.

FORENSIC ACCOUNTING

What you need: Finding financial crimes is one of those jobs that you'd never guess had its own school. But it does, and having an accounting background will help you to thrive.

Typical salary: The 2017 median salary was 77,920 dollars with highs hovering in the mid 100,000 dollar range.

Nick's take: With the advent of criminal hacking, financial crimes are becoming more prevalent by the day. Good guys with a nose for numbers will be wise to get into this profession.

FUNERAL / MORTUARY

What you need: Nothing specific, just fearlessness and a good heart.

Typical salary: The 2017 median income for a funeral director was 53,590 dollars. Grave digging isn't a lucrative profession, with the median salary clocking in at 23,740 dollars. So if you want into this industry, shoot for the top.

Nick's take: This is an uncomfortable vocation, and it takes a special soul to partake, let alone succeed. But if you're that special soul, you could make a nice living while making the world a better place.

GARDENING AND LANDSCAPE DESIGN

What you need: As is the case with a florist, a good eye and an interest in nature is a good place to start, as is an apprenticeship.

Typical salary: The 2015 median salary for a landscape architect was 63,810 dollars.

Nick's take: There's far more to landscaping than cutting grass. There are plenty of well-off families who will appreciate—and pay good money—for an expert to make their lawn the best on the block.

GRAPHIC DESIGN

What you need: Simple: skills with a variety of design software and an artistic bent.

Typical salary: Considering the wide range of client needs, the 2017 salaries varied from 48,700 to 170,230 dollars.

Nick's take: This is one of the fastest growing industries in the country—it's projected to be one of the top five growers in the next ten years—so while the schooling is distinctly college-like, it'll likely be worth your while.

GUNSMITHING

What you need: A gun license and an apprenticeship are essential.

Typical salary: In 2017, the median pay was 40,175 dollars, topping out at sixty thousand dollars or more.

Nick's take: Between 2005 and 2015, small arms manufacturing increased 208 percent. Somebody has to fix all those guns, right?

HAIR STYLIST

What you need: This is a labor of love, so if you want to cut hair for a living, you have to *really* want it.

Typical salary: In 2017, the median salary was 30,490 dollars, with a high end of 50,600 dollars.

Nick's take: In and of itself, this isn't a particularly lucrative way to go, but if you develop a clientele, you could get on the path to hanging out your own shingle.

HEALTH CARE MANAGEMENT / HEALTH SERVICES ADMINISTRATION

What you need: Considering this covers everything from medical malpractice management, to nursing administration, to running an assisted living facility, knowledge of the industry and a relatively focused direction is key.

Typical salary: There's plenty of money to be earned here, as demonstrated by the 2017 range of 111,680 to 176,130 dollars.

Nick's take: As is the case with every arena of healthcare, an additional satisfaction of helping others is part and parcel.

HEAVY EQUIPMENT

What you need: Being that you'll have to learn about heavy vehicle maintenance, construction machinery operation, and mining vehicle operation, you'd better know about driving. A commercial driver's license is also needed.

Typical salary: In 2017, the median salary was 50,860 dollars, with the top earners taking in 82,280 dollars.

Nick's take: With an expected growth level of 12 percent through 2026, this could be a great path to follow.

HIGH PERFORMANCE ENGINES

What you need: You probably can't go from tinkering with a carburetor to working on a racecar engine, so an in-depth knowledge of cars is essential.

Typical salary: This is the kind of industry in which you have to work your way up. In 2017, newbies were earning 40,283 dollars, while experts were taking in 102,162 dollars.

Nick's take: In terms of car repair, this is the top of the food chain. There aren't a ton of available positions, so you'd better be really, really good.

HIGH SCHOOL DIPLOMA PREPARATION

What you need: Logically enough, a high school diploma.

Typical salary: In 2016, adult literacy/GED teachers took in a median salary of forty-four thousand dollars.

Nick's take: If you have a burning desire to teach, but not a burning desire to babysit, you could thrive in this industry.

HISTORY

What you need: It's counterintuitive to think that a history school doesn't require a college degree. But, well, it doesn't, just high school. Go figure.

Typical salary: These are generalized schools that lead to a multitude of specific positions. As is the case with this sort of industry, there's no such thing as a typical salary.

Nick's take: The positions run the gamut from history researcher to national monument curator, so if you're any kind of history buff, you'll find something to tickle your fancy.

HOME AUTOMATION

What you need: Installing home consumer electronic systems is considerably more difficult than it sounds, so hopefully you will have done your homework before diving into schooling.

Typical salary: In 2017, this growth industry had a median salary of 47,870 dollars, with the top earners taking in 76,720 dollars.

Nick's take: Being that you'll install everything from home security systems to surround sound, you'll become a well-rounded electronics expert, so this could lead to bigger and better jobs, as well as your own business.

HOME INSPECTION

What you need: A little knowledge about a lot of things, i.e., real estate, electronics, construction, and decoration.

Typical salary: In 2017, the average salary was 62,620 dollars, with experienced inspectors taking in over six figures.

Nick's take: Think about your friends who have bought lousy houses. They probably didn't use a quality inspector…or they might not have used one at all. This is an important job with a ton of responsibility, so you'd better be able to carry the load. But in the end, it'll be worth it, because of the steady work and nice salary.

HOMELAND SECURITY

What you need: A military background…for which a college degree is far from necessary.

Typical salary: With positions in the TSA, FEMA, the Secret Service, and the Coast Guard—among *many* others—the salaries are all over the place. But the money is uniformly good, and the benefits are phenomenal.

Nick's take: The United States is looking for a few good men and women…actually, more than a few. There are plenty of jobs for a talented, driven sort to choose from, jobs with plenty of growth potential, and jobs that can last up until retirement. (More about this in a few dozen pages.)

HOSPITALITY

What you need: This may seem simplistic, but if you're going to be, say, a travel agent, knowledge of the world is a must.

Typical salary: The 2017 salary range was impressive, with a median number of eighty-two thousand dollars. Six-figure salaries are a regular thing.

Nick's take: This is a 1.5 trillion dollar industry. Enough said.

HOSPITALITY MANAGEMENT

What you need: If you're not an outgoing person who enjoys the company of others, don't bother. Introverts don't make great cruise ship directors.

Typical salary: In 2017, lodging managers took in a median salary of 51,840 dollars, while food service managers brought home 50,820 dollars. Each position—as well as the numerous others that fall under this umbrella—has six-figure potential.

Nick's take: People persons (or is it people peoples?) could live a happy life at the top end of the service industry.

HOTEL MANAGEMENT

What you need: It's all about polish. If you don't clean up well, chances of succeeding in this competitive industry are slim.

Typical salary: Here's something to which you can aspire: Experienced, quality hotel general managers have a median salary—*a median salary!*—of 100,410 dollars.

Nick's take: Of all the jobs on this list, the fun-to-money ratio here is about as high as it gets.

HUMAN RESOURCES

What you need: This job requires as much patience and thick skin as any job listed. If you don't like complaints, take a pass.

Typical salary: This is a lucrative profession, as proven by the fact that in 2017, HR assistants had a median salary of 40,700 dollars, while compensation and benefits managers took in 130,010 dollars.

Nick's take: I'm not going to lie: human resources sounds like a thoroughly difficult task. But if you can crack it, you might well be set for life.

HVAC (HEATING, VENTILATION, AND AIR CONDITIONING)

What you need: You can head into HVAC school a blank slate, but you'll do considerably better if you're good with tools, and if you've had an apprenticeship.

Typical salary: In 2017, the median salary was 47,080 dollars, with the top earners pulling down seventy-five thousand or more dollars.

Nick's take: This is another position that has job security and decent wages. Home owners, condo owners, and apartment renters will always have mechanical breakdowns of some sort, so not only will you be busy, but you'll be beloved when you come by to fix the air conditioner on a ninety-five-degree day.

INDUSTRIAL TECHNOLOGY

What you need: Nothing specific, but you'd better know something about the guts of electronic devices.

Typical salary: There's money to be had here, as demonstrated by the top-end salaries for industrial machine mechanics (77,540 dollars) and building maintenance technicians (61,720 dollars).

Nick's take: You don't think about the fact that somebody has to fix those big machines that keep skyscrapers up and running. It takes an individualistic skillset to handle that gig, thus the nice job security and solid salary.

INTERIOR DESIGN

What you need: This isn't just about making things pretty. In addition to knowing how to beautify houses and retail spaces, you have to have business acumen and quality interpersonal skills.

Typical salary: In 2017, the salaries ranged from 51,500 to 93,780 dollars.

Nick's take: Like most of the arts-based vocations that offer trade schools, this one will be fulfilling to creative types… plus it could lead to a solo business venture, of which I'm a huge fan.

INTERNATIONAL BUSINESS AND TRADE

What you need: If you're going to succeed in this industry—and it's far from easy—you'd better do a whole bunch of legwork on your own. You can't saunter into these schools without a good idea of how business works.

Typical salary: There are a lot of big numbers here, with an international operations manager taking in a 2017 top salary of 156,580 dollars. Even an international paralegal can earn 81,800 dollars.

Nick's take: If you can focus and work your butt off, this schooling gives you the opportunity to become a true titan of industry. But it's all up to you.

INTERNET MARKETING

What you need: In-depth social media savvy and a good handle on SEO is a must.

Typical salary: In 2017, a top web analytics expert could rake in up to 74,300 dollars. I'm confident to say that by the time you read this book, that number will have amped up exponentially.

Nick's take: Every company that has a website—and, at this point, that's pretty much every company anywhere—needs a web marketer...or an email marketer...or a social media marketer...or an analytics person. We're talking opportunities galore.

JEWELRY REPAIR AND GOLDSMITH

What you need: If you're not good with your hands, or can't handle small tools, all the study in the world won't help you succeed here.

Typical salary: In 2017, jewelry repair experts and goldsmiths alike had median incomes around forty-five thousand dollars.

Nick's take: Another profession that, while not scintillating in and of itself, can lead to business ownership.

JOURNALISM

What you need: An inquisitive mind, a nose for news, the ability to put a sentence together, and sheer doggedness. Easy, right?

Typical salary: What with the internet, print media, and televised media, you can't come close to nailing down a typical salary. But if you can deliver the content, regardless of the platform, international media companies and high-profile book publishers might come knocking at your door.

Nick's take: Journalism is a labor of love that could become a goldmine. But you get out what you put in, so put in a whole lot.

LASER TECHNICIAN

What you need: A steady hand and a passion for skin.

Typical salary: The top money for laser techs in 2017 clocked in at just under sixty thousand dollars, while newcomers to the industry were earning just over thirty-five thousand dollars.

Nick's take: There will always be people looking to remove back hair and tattoos, so if you like prettifying the human body in myriad ways, this might be the profession for you.

LEGAL ASSISTANT

What you need: Nothing concrete, but a cursory knowledge of the law sure helps.

Typical salary: The 2015 median salary for a legal assistant was 48,810 dollars.

Nick's take: The gap between a garden-variety administrative assistant and a legal assistant, while not insurmountable, is wide enough to more than justify specialized schooling.

And if you're a good legal assistant, well, there are a lot of lawyers in this country.

LIVE MUSIC PRODUCTION

What you need: If you're not a music fanatic, you should probably consider another gig.

Typical salary: In 2017, the median salary was 34,946 dollars

Nick's take: This isn't a lucrative job, truth be told, but if you're a musician who isn't getting enough gigs, or a music nut who likes going to clubs eight nights a week, this might be the ideal way to spend your professional life.

LIVE SOUND ENGINEERING

What you need: Good ears and a working knowledge of music hardware and software.

Typical salary: In 2018, the median salary was 33,074 dollars.

Nick's take: As is the case with a live music producer, this isn't a job for somebody looking for big bucks—although if you do a good job at the small clubs, there's always the possibility that a band will fall in love with you and take you on the road. Granted, there isn't huge money in that either, but you'll be happy.

LOCKSMITHING

What you need: A steady hand for repairing those locks.

Typical salary: Believe it or not, there's decent money in locksmithing, with a 2018 median salary of 50,126 dollars.

Nick's take: There will always be broken locks, thus there will always be jobs.

LPN / LVN

What you need: No specific skills necessary to begin schooling, but if you're going to become a licensed practical nurse (LPN) or licensed vocational nurse (LVN), you need passion and compassion.

Typical salary: Salaries vary widely from state to state, but the median figure in 2017 was 45,710 dollars.

Nick's take: I have a dear friend who's an LPN, and she works her butt off, and there's always some sort of drama going on at her hospital, but she loves it and wouldn't change a thing.

MAKEUP ARTIST

What you need: If you're going to thrive, you'd best have some hands-on experience. A professional-looking portfolio of your work sure wouldn't hurt either.

Typical salary: You won't make great money right out of school, but if you hustle, you could find yourself pulling down something in the 2017 range of 69,310 to 127,030 dollars.

Nick's take: This is a booming industry, with a generally wealthy and loyal clientele. If you comport yourself in a professional manner—and if you can make your clients glow—you'll have work galore.

MANICURIST

What you need: If you can't do a competent nail job before entering school, you should probably enter a different kind of school.

Typical salary: In 2017, the salary ranged from 23,230 to 33,050 dollars.

Nick's take: You won't be able to earn a great living as just a nail technician, but if you're good, and if you're a hard worker, opening your own salon isn't out of the realm of possibility.

MARINE AND WATERCRAFT REPAIR

What you need: There's more to fixing boats than one might expect, so study up before starting school, or you might find yourself behind before you even start.

Typical salary: In 2017, the median salary was 41,350 dollars.

Nick's take: There are a surprisingly large, diverse number of positions under this umbrella—we're talking boat rigger, dealership technician, gelcoat and fiberglass technician, marina service manager, marine electrician, marine parts sales associate, marine air conditioning and refrigerator technician, and rig shop manager—so these schools are more than a little engaging.

MARKETING

What you need: Goals, goals, goals. You want to begin your marketing life with an idea of where you're headed, as there are numerous directions you can take.

Typical salary: There are a ton of different marketing disciplines, so there are a ton of salaries, with a 2017 range of 53,208 to 123,880 dollars.

Nick's take: I have a friend who attended marketing school—not college, just a marketing school—and is now CMO of an international tech company. That won't happen for everybody…but it could happen for you.

MASSAGE THERAPY

What you need: Strong hands—very, very strong hands.

Typical salary: There are plenty of venues for massage therapists, thus the wide 2017 salary range of 39,680 to 74,870 dollars.

Nick's take: This is a tough school—there are at least a dozen different types of massage you'll need to learn—but you'll have the freedom to work for yourself or for, say, a spa or a hotel, or a chiropractor. There are lots of options; lots of opportunities.

MECHANICAL ENGINEERING TECHNICIAN

What you need: Good eyesight, a steady hand, and a good memory, because you'll be dealing with a whole lot of different machinery (and, of course, an apprenticeship).

Typical salary: In 2018, mechanical engineers were pulling down a median salary of 73,016 dollars.

Nick's take: This is high-end mechanical work that requires patience and meticulousness. You can't just *do* this. You have to *work* at this. But the money is there, so it'll be worth it.

MEDIA ARTS

What you need: Know all aspects of the media: film, television, print, online (and not just a little bit).

Typical salary: In 2017, multimedia artists were taking in a median salary of 73,700 dollars, with the high-end workers earning 103,510 dollars.

Nick's take: These are terrific catchall schools that offer classes in everything from app development, to 3D modeling, to graphic design. But they have a distinctly college-like atmosphere, so be prepared.

MEDICAL ADMINISTRATIVE ASSISTANT

What you need: Terrific interpersonal skills, a knowledge of office software, and a curiosity about the medical profession.

Typical salary: In 2017, you were looking at a salary range from 35,870 to 50,340 dollars.

Nick's take: This isn't just about answering phones and booking appointments. You need to know about medical records, medical coding, and transcribing doctor's recordings. But quality medical A.A.'s are in demand, so you'll always work.

MEDICAL ASSISTANT

What you need: A high school diploma, and, preferably, a knowledge of biology, chemistry, and anatomy.

Typical salary: The 2016 median salary was 31,540 dollars, with the top 10 percent earning 45,310 dollars.

Nick's take: As is the case with all hands-on, non-doctor, non-nurse healthcare positions, there isn't huge money, but there is huge personal fulfillment…not to mention great benefits.

MEDICAL BILLING AND CODING

What you need: Same thing as Medical Administrative Assistant. But this is wildly different schooling.

Typical salary: In 2017, the median salary was 46,899 dollars, with a high end of 60,305 dollars.

Nick's take: If you're going to simplify it, this is kind of like the technical end of medical assistant, without having to deal with patients. So if you like detail but don't like people, this could be ideal.

MEDICAL LAB TECHNICIAN

What you need: A high tolerance for all bodily fluids and solids.

Typical salary: The 2017 median salary was 55,230 dollars, with a top end of 79,530 dollars.

Nick's take: Chances are you don't like getting blood drawn, which means you might not like drawing blood. This explains the nice salary.

MEDICAL OFFICE ADMINISTRATION

What you need: Same thing as Medical Assistant and Medical Billing and Coding. But, again, this is wildly different schooling.

Typical salary: The 2017 median salary for a medical secretary was 35,800 dollars, while a medical service manager was pulling in just under one hundred thousand dollars.

Nick's take: Depending on your level of interest, this could be a job or it could be a career. Regardless, there will always be doctor's offices and health insurance companies, so you'll always work.

MEDICAL RECEPTIONIST

What you need: A typical receptionist skill set, with a curiosity about the medical profession.

Typical salary: The 2017 median salary was 30,670 dollars, topping out at 40,880 dollars.

Nick's take: There isn't much earning potential here, but if you're looking for an A.A. position with more job security than your average A.A. gig, here you go.

MEDICAL TRANSCRIPTION

What you need: A quality vocabulary, good spelling skills, and the ability to type at least sixty words per minute.

Typical salary: In 2014, the median salary was 34,890 dollars.

Nick's take: The transcriptionist for this very book earned herself some good money. This obviously isn't a medical book, but the point is that quality transcribers, regardless of the industry, can easily find freelance work.

MOBILE APPLICATION DEVELOPMENT

What you need: Creativity, computer skills, and hustle. The first two are hugely important, but don't underestimate number three, as there are a whole lot of good developers out there.

Typical salary: In 2017, quality developers earned six figures, with a low end of 106,710 dollars and a high end of 160,100 dollars.

Nick's take: As of mid-2016, over sixty-five billion apps had been downloaded from Google Play alone. If you develop well, you will work, and you will thrive.

MOTORCYCLE REPAIR

What you need: As is generally the case with all vehicle repair, an apprenticeship is highly recommended.

Typical salary: In 2017, newbies were taking in 11.17 dollars an hour, while experienced mechanics earned as much as fifty thousand dollars per year.

Nick's take: There aren't a whole lot of motorcycle repair specialists out there, which is fortunate for the aspiring repair person, as there are opportunities at dealerships, repair shops, and manufacturers. And if you're really good—and I'm not kidding here—you can join a motorcycle racing team!

MUSIC PRODUCTION AND RECORDING ARTS

What you need: A great ear, some musical skills, and a background with recording software such as Pro Tools, Ableton, and Apple Logic Pro X.

Typical salary: In 2017, recording engineers were taking in an average of 68,180 dollars, while top producers earned as much as 189,870 dollars.

Nick's take: Lots of musicians have their own home studios, so this is a competitive industry. But if you're good, you'll work, and if you work, you'll earn.

NETWORKING AND SYSTEM ADMINISTRATION

What you need: You can't be a casual computer person and thrive in these schools. This is tough stuff, but it'll take you places.

Typical salary: Quality networkers are in huge demand, as proven by the average 2017 salary of 86,340 dollars, not to mention the top end of 130,200 dollars.

Nick's take: This is among the least glamorous jobs in the computer world, but if you have the computer chops and the desire to get a company's network up and running—and *keep* it running—you'll do quite well for yourself.

NURSING

What you need: Nursing is all about the desire to help others. Anything else can be learned in school or on the job, but if the compassion isn't there, you simply won't thrive.

Typical salary: What with all the different nursing disciplines, it's little surprise that the 2017 salary ranged from 48,690 to 102,700 dollars.

Nick's take: Nurses will work and nurses will earn. And, frankly, if you do well in nursing school—and continue your quality work on the job—you'll be more treasured than a goodly number of doctors.

OCCUPATIONAL THERAPY

What you need: Some knowledge of the human body and a heap of patience.

Typical salary: The 2017 salaries ranged from 59,470 to 80,320 dollars.

Nick's take: There are plenty of venues where you can help people get back on their feet (literally and figuratively), i.e., hospitals, nursing homes, mental health centers, and all levels of schools. You will rarely, if ever, be without a job and a decent salary.

OFFICE ADMINISTRATOR

What you need: A pleasant demeanor, attention to detail, and expertise in office computer software. The ability to read your boss' mind wouldn't hurt, but that's highly unlikely.

Typical salary: The 2017 hourly rates ranged from 14.25 to 78.60 dollars.

Nick's take: There are a lot of office administrators out there who haven't attended this particular trade school, so this will give you the opportunity to have a leg up on the competition and pull in that 78.60 dollars per hour rather than the 14.25 dollars per hour.

PARALEGAL

What you need: A working knowledge of what paralegals do and how they do it. This is a competitive industry, and only the prepared will thrive.

Typical salary: The average 2017 private sector salary was 49,500 dollars, with government paralegals taking in a median of 62,400 dollars.

Nick's take: There are approximately fifty thousand law firms in the country, all of which need multiple paralegals. The opportunity is there, but if you're going to stick, you'd better be good.

PARAMEDIC / EMT

What you need: A driver's license and an unshakeable desire to help others.

Typical salary: In 2017, the median salary was 33,380 dollars, with the top 10 percent earning 56,990 dollars.

Nick's take: This is a growth industry—we're talking a projected 15 percent growth between 2016 and 2026—but it's a tough gig, so if you think you can handle life-or-death emergencies, go for it.

PATIENT CARE TECHNICIAN

What you need: You'll be working mostly in nursing homes, so if you can't handle the aging process, you need not apply.

Typical salary: In 2017, the average hourly salary was 12.81 dollars.

Nick's take: There isn't a whole lot of money here, but the on-the-job training with real live doctors and patients is invaluable, and the fact that you get to help those who are suffering is magical.

PERFORMING ARTS

What you need: An in-depth knowledge of the entertainment industry, a bulletproof ego, and a killer work ethic.

Typical salary: There isn't anything *close* to a typical salary. In 2017, an inexperienced actor could work for free, while a top theater director could earn 91.28 dollars an hour.

Nick's take: For many, a general performing arts school is more useful than, say, an acting-specific school. A well-rounded entertainment skillset could offer more opportunity to work, and in the entertainment world, it's all about the work.

PERSONAL TRAINER

What you need: Strength, stamina, and the ability to create healthy meals day in and day out. Without those, this is a non-starter.

Typical salary: In 2017, the hourly wage ranged between 21.02 and 35.83 dollars.

Nick's take: This is an appealing job for the entrepreneurial-minded workout maven, as you can start your own personal training business without much in the way of overhead. All you need is a living space, a phone, some exercise mats, weights, and a couple of workout machines.

PHARMACY TECHNICIAN

What you need: A good memory, because there are a lot of prescription drugs you'll have to deal with.

Typical salary: In 2017, the median salary was 31,750 dollars, with the top 10 percent bringing in 46,980 dollars.

Nick's take: A pharmacist is often just as important as a doctor, so this is a serious profession for serious people. One of my friends is an excellent pharmacist—and has been for over a decade—and she's never been without a job.

PHLEBOTOMY

What you need: This is a specialized area, that specialty being blood. So you'd better be able to tolerate the red stuff.

Typical salary: In 2017, the median salary was 33,670 dollars, topping out at 48,030 dollars.

Nick's take: Remember that time you went to the doctor, and the tech that drew your blood was a jerk? That person (and all the people like them) probably doesn't work in this industry anymore, so the opportunities will be there.

PHOTOGRAPHY

What you need: A good eye, the ability to operate a camera other than the one on your iPhone, and an in-depth knowledge of the industry, because there's more to it than you might think.

Typical salary: In 2017, the median salary was 41,940 dollars.

Nick's take: Sure, weddings need professional photographers, but so do businesses, the government, and, of course, advertisers. A photography school can help you diversify, and if you diversify, you'll probably have a fun, profitable professional life.

PHYSICAL THERAPY AID

What you need: A wide array of health and healing know-how, everything from massage to anatomy.

Typical salary: The 2017 median wage was 57,430 dollars, with a high end of 79,380 dollars.

Nick's take: There's a reason for the hefty salary. A quality PT maven has to be a trainer, a doctor, a psychologist, and an administrator, all wrapped up into one. Best of all, there are PT storefronts popping up everywhere, so there's work to be had.

PLUMBING

What you need: There's far more to plumbing than one might expect, so an apprenticeship with an expert is essential.

Typical salary: The 2016 median wage was 51,450, with a high point of 90,530 dollars.

Nick's take: As much as any trade, plumbing comes with a stigma—most think of the job as just unclogging drains—but the fact of the matter is, you learn about, among other things, construction, welding, and design. It's a growth industry, and it often leads to owning a business. This is a quality profession, period.

POLICE / LAW ENFORCEMENT

What you need: Fearlessness.

Typical salary: This sort of schooling can lead to everything from beat cop, to correctional officer, to security guard, to emergency management director. Salaries are all over the place, but in 2017, experienced police offers were topping one hundred thousand dollars, so the earning potential is there.

Nick's take: I'm friendly with enough law enforcement officials to know that this profession isn't pretty. It can be scary, and boring, and frustrating, but also satisfying and lucrative, so if you want to stop the bad guys, please, we beg you, go for it!

PROJECT MANAGEMENT

What you need: Interpersonal skills and the ability to simultaneously take big picture and small picture views of your work. Not an easy balance.

Typical salary: In 2013, construction project managers earned between 70,978 and 87,560 dollars, while managers with additional schooling had a median salary of 108,000 dollars.

Nick's take: Engineering on any level isn't easy, but when you add in the fact that you'll have to lead a team, well, now you know why these folks take home a hefty paycheck.

PROPERTY MANAGEMENT

What you need: Knowledge of everything on this list: mechanics, bookkeeping, administration, plumbing, and so on.

Typical salary: The 2017 median salary was 72,370 dollars, with a top shelf of 163,480 dollars.

Nick's take: Property management isn't the kind of profession you'd assume would require schooling, but when you think about how many hats a manager has to wear, it makes sense…as does the impressive salary.

PUBLIC RELATIONS

What you need: This is a do-it-all gig, so you'd better come armed with a wide range of skills: writing, business acumen, traditional media know-how, social media savvy, and, above all, polish.

Typical salary: Good PR people—emphasis on good—are in demand, as proven by the 2017 salary range of 67,990 to 112,260 dollars.

Nick's take: What with the potential to work with the rich and famous, this may seem like a glamorous job, but it's cutthroat, so if you decide to dive in, you'd better be ready to go for it.

RADIO / TELEVISION BROADCASTING

What you need: A good voice, a good camera presence, technical knowhow, and the ability to work well with others. Leave your ego at home, whether you're behind or in front of the camera or the microphone.

Typical salary: In 2017, broadcast technicians had a median salary of 46,730 dollars, announcers clocked in at 47,630 dollars, camera operators brought home 61,530 dollars, and producers and directors took in 90,770 dollars.

Nick's take: Yes, for many, the internet is their primary place to go for news, but there is and always will be television and radio (probably), so while the competition is tough, the cream will rise to the top and land a quality position.

REAL ESTATE

What you need: An eye for property and knowledge of your neighborhood is essential. But you'd better have a go-getter, entrepreneurial spirit, because if you're going to thrive here, it's all on you.

Typical salary: Brokers work primarily on commission, so the sky is the limit. But in 2017, real estate assessors were taking in a median salary of 60,830 dollars, with mortgage brokers not far behind at fifty-eight thousand or more.

Nick's take: I have a friend who, after washing out as an actor and a model, got his real estate license and is now—no exaggeration—a billionaire. That said, he's one of the hardest workers I've ever met, so he earned it. And so can you!

RESPIRATORY THERAPIST

What you need: A high school diploma or GED and a cursory knowledge of the respiratory system.

Typical salary: In 2016, the median salary was 58,670 dollars.

Nick's take: With opportunities at hospitals, nursing homes, sleep labs, and research facilities, there's no shortage of positions for a relatively small work force.

RESTAURANT MANAGEMENT

What you need: Hands-on restaurant experience—e.g., server, bartender, line cook—isn't required, but it will make your schooling much, much easier.

Typical salary: In 2018, the average base pay for a restaurant manager was 52,115 dollars, with high-end general managers pulling in salaries in the low-one-hundred-thousand-dollar range.

Nick's take: This job isn't for the faint of heart. You'll put in crazy hours, you'll deal with more big personalities than you can imagine, and you'll be on your feet 90 percent of the day. But if you love the restaurant world—and there are plenty of you who do—you could be thrilled with this life.

SKIN CARE

What you need: A strong background in cosmetics and beauty supplies.

Typical salary: In 2017, skin care specialists were taking in an average of 30,270 dollars.

Nick's take: This schooling also offers classes on how to become an esthetician, so make sure you get in on that, because the more knowledge you have at your disposal, the more money you'll have at your disposal.

SMALL ENGINE REPAIR

What you need: If you've read this far, you're well aware that if you go into any kind of repair field, an apprenticeship is key.

Typical salary: The 2018 median salary was 40,140 dollars.

Nick's take: Hey, somebody has to fix lawnmowers and powerboat engines. There aren't that many people doing it, so why don't you take a crack?

SOLAR ENERGY

What you need: This is a difficult discipline, so passion is crucial, as is showing up to school with a working knowledge of solar power.

Typical salary: There are literally dozens of jobs that fall under this umbrella, from installers to operators to maintenance managers. In 2016, the yearly numbers ran the gamut from thirty-seven thousand to one hundred thousand dollars.

Nick's take: With two hundred fifty thousand or more solar power workers in the field in 2017, this is a booming, diverse market, and could be financially and personally fulfilling for the ecologically-oriented.

SOMMELIER

What you need: A serious knowledge of wine…*really* serious. Casual sippers need not apply.

Typical salary: In 2017, newcomers to the field were earning around 30,000 dollars, but experts were taking in between 80,000 and 160,000 thousand dollars.

Nick's take: Food and drink culture is huge in America, so the competition for these jobs is fierce. But if you're patient, hard working, and can hone your wine craft, you could get paid quite well for doing something you truly love. And isn't that a goal for everybody?

SPECIAL EFFECTS

What you need: An insanely good imagination, an encyclopedic knowledge of the *Star Wars* canon, and expertise at pretty much every kind of graphics software.

Typical salary: The average base pay for a visual effects artist in 2017 was 94,720 dollars.

Nick's take: There are probably hundreds of thousands of high school seniors who would choose an SFX school over, well, anything...*but they might not know these schools exist.* So spread the word, and give these kids a chance to earn an awesome living.

SPORTS MEDICINE

What you need: Ideally some athletic prowess, as well as cursory knowledge of human anatomy.

Typical salary: Sports medicine is an umbrella term, covering a number of different disciplines, which means a number of different salaries. For example, in 2017, a physical therapist aid pulled in an average of 27,910 dollars, while a coaching assistant topped out at 75,400 dollars.

Nick's take: There are thousands of people who would be thrilled with a job that combines fitness, teaching, and maintaining a healthy lifestyle.

STERILE PROCESSING

What you need: An attention to detail, the ability to work quickly and accurately, and the desire to keep hospitals from getting infected.

Typical salary: In 2017, the median salary was 35,370 dollars.

Nick's take: This is one of those jobs that, unless you're currently doing it, you probably didn't know existed before this moment...but, well, *somebody* has to sterilize *everything* at the hospital. This is a really important position, and there's plenty of opportunity.

SURGICAL TECHNOLOGIST

What you need: See "Sterile Processing," above.

Typical salary: The 2017 median salary was 46,310 dollars, with top earners taking in 67,000 dollars or more.

Nick's take: Known by the less fancy term "scrub tech," there aren't too many of these folks out there, so if you succeed in your schooling, you shouldn't have trouble landing and keeping a job.

SUSTAINABLE BUSINESS

What you need: A burning desire to make the planet work better.

Typical salary: In 2017, sustainability coordinators were averaging 46,316 dollars, while sustainability directors took in 102,365 dollars. The remaining positions (manager, consultant, specialist) clocked in around sixty thousand dollars.

Nick's take: There aren't a whole lot of folks who have the combination of scientific *and* business skill sets to thrive in these positions, so if you jump on this early, you can carve out a nice life for yourself.

ULTRASOUND TECHNOLOGIST

What you need: A working knowledge of the human body, as well as the same thing all healthcare providers need—quality bedside manner.

Typical salary: The 2017 median wage was 71,410 dollars.

Nick's take: You know those imaging centers that seem to be popping up in your local strip malls? Well, somebody needs to work there, and somebody needs to earn those 71,410 dollars per year, so why shouldn't that somebody be you?

UNDERWATER WELDING

What you need: A commercial diving certificate and a complete welding training.

Typical salary: An average salary is difficult to calculate, as most underwater welders are freelancers and are thus paid on a project-by-project basis. But the majority of people in this field take in between one hundred thousand and two hundred thousand dollars a year.

Nick's take: I didn't know underwater welding was a thing, nor did I know schools where you can learn underwater welding were a thing. But these things add up to a whole lot of money, so it might be a good idea to dive in. (See what I did there? Again?)

VETERINARY TECHNICIAN

What you need: The same basic qualities you'd need to be a registered nurse, as well as a love of all animals. (It's fine to be a dog person or a cat person at home, but when you're on the job here, no animal favoritism allowed.)

Typical salary: The 2017 median salary was 33,400 dollars, with the top 10 percent earners pulling down 49,350 dollars.

Nick's take: There isn't huge earning potential here, but if you are an animal lover, this will likely be a fulfilling job, regardless of your paycheck's size.

VIDEO GAME DESIGN

What you need: Come to the table with the ability to rudimentarily create and execute game narratives. If you can't imagine a video game before beginning this schooling, you likely won't succeed.

Typical salary: The 2018 average salary was 88,270 dollars.

Nick's take: Hopefully your game-obsessed child has learned enough about the industry through playing that they'll be able to take the leap, because this could be a financially rewarding profession…as well as the fulfillment of a dream.

VIDEO PRODUCTION

What you need: A good eye, an idea of what does and doesn't work on television and in the movies, and "stick-toitiveness," because this is one helluva competitive field.

Typical salary: There is a wide range of on-and-offline jobs, which is reflected in the wide 2017 salary range of 58,260 to 189,270 dollars.

Nick's take: There are thousands of websites in need of quality video content, so production is more sought after than ever.

VISUAL ARTS

What you need: The ability to create something beautiful with both your hands and your computer.

Typical salary: The wide range of positions comes with a wide range of salaries. For instance, in 2017, a top illustrator pulled in 102,000 dollars, while a top art director made 107,000 dollars.

Nick's take: This isn't about drawing pictures. This is about advertising. This is about making compelling video. This is about utilizing your artistic soul to create a happy, lucrative life for yourself.

WEB DESIGN AND DEVELOPMENT

What you need: More software, hardware, design, and marketplace knowledge than your competition. And being that there are a lot of web designers out there, that means you'd better get on the stick.

Typical salary: The average salary in 2018 was 48,924 dollars.

Nick's take: Admittedly, designers were far more in demand as recently as five years ago, but with the advent of DIY webpage companies like Wix.com, anybody with average computers skills can slap together a respectable site. But companies both big and small still need professional sites developed and maintained, so if you're good, the opportunity is there.

WEDDING CONSULTANT

What you need: This is a competitive field, so you'd better head off to school with a good eye, the ability to juggle multiple tasks, and a patience for bridezillas.

Typical salary: Because different consultants specialize in different-sized weddings, the 2017 salary ranged between 48,290 and 82,980 dollars.

Nick's take: I have a friend who parlayed her freelance wedding planning career into a massive event planning business, so don't dismiss this vocation as frivolous, not for a minute.

WELDING

What you need: Say it with me now: *an apprenticeship.*

Typical salary: The average 2017 salary was 43,410 dollars, with the top earners taking in 63,170 dollars.

Nick's take: There isn't a huge demand for welders—there's only a 5 percent job growth predicted up through 2026—but if you're dedicated and talented, you'll work.

WIND ENERGY

What you need: Nothing specific, but some success in your high school science classes sure wouldn't hurt.

Typical salary: In 2017, the average salary for a wind turbine tech was 56,680 dollars, with the top 10 percent earning as much as 80,170 dollars.

Nick's take: There could be as much as a 30 percent job growth in this industry before 2030, and right now, relatively speaking, the field is wide open, so get in while the getting is good.

X-RAY / RADIOLOGIC TECHNICIAN

What you need: See pretty much every other medical profession on this list.

Typical salary: In 2017, x-ray techs were earning an average of 38,585 dollars, while radiologic techs took in an average of 58,440 dollars.

Nick's take: What with the need for x-ray techs at doctor's offices, immediate care facilities, hospitals, physical therapy outlets, and so on, this position is more in demand than ever. And the work will always be there for qualified individuals, because medical science still hasn't figured out a way to gauge the severity of an internal injury without a machine.

There are a whole lot of vocational choices here—many of which you hadn't considered, and many of which you didn't know had educational facilities—so take your time before making a decision.

Before enrolling, be sure and do your research. Visit your potential school. Audit a class. Talk to somebody who works in the profession. Finding people to interview won't be a problem, because anybody who likes their job loves to blab about it.

The most important thing is to choose something about which you're passionate, or, at the very least, something you can tolerate. If you've read to this point, there's somebody in your life who's averse to schooling—for that matter, you yourself may be that anti-college person—so if education is going to be pursued, it should be something that offers the opportunity for professional success, financial stability, and personal happiness.

16

In 1981, the United States Army began an ad campaign with the slogan "Be all you can be." The campaign included commercials, t-shirts, posters, billboards; the works. It was a creative triumph for the Army, so much so that in December 1999, *Advertising Age* magazine awarded it the eighteenth spot on their list of top one hundred ad campaigns of the twentieth century.

Apparently N.W. Ayer, the agency that created the campaign, was all that it could be.

Those ads made the military look awesome: *enlist and you could learn how to defend your country, and crawl through barbed wire, and cover yourself in camouflage and mud, and return home to the proud, awaiting hands of your loved ones.*

Those are indeed wonderful reasons to enlist, but one of the best reasons—especially in light of skyrocketing tuition costs—is that the military will educate you.

If you join the United States Army, Navy, Air Force, or Marines, you have access to a number of programs that will enable you to afford college, should that be the direction you'd like to go.

Tuition Assistance, for instance, covers 100 percent of tuition—that's the whole enchilada, people—if you meet all the requirements. Then there's the Top-Up program, and the Post-9/11 GI Bill, and the Montgomery GI Bill for active military and veterans, as well as various amounts of federal aid and scholarships.

There's a reason military personnel are granted these opportunities. The gallant men and women of our Armed Services, past and present, have spilt blood, lost limbs, and paid the ultimate price to defend and protect the greatest human virtue of them all: freedom. More than that, American warriors are in a league of their own. Our warriors are the kind inclined to re-enlist after losing a limb or voluntarily absorbing the blast of a detonated suicide vest to ensure their teammates can complete their mission. Other armies may outnumber ours, but none have our resolve or fearlessness.

Also, Uncle Sam wants you to be smart. Because that's how the military gets bigger, better, and stronger: brains.

My friend Frank is a perfect example of how the military machine can work for somebody who didn't have an educational direction.

Frank grew up in a working class town outside of Pittsburgh, where he felt like an outsider. "I wasn't into the same things everybody else was. And those things were drinking beer and listening to shitty metal. I was all about weightlifting." (Dave, for the record, is still all about weightlifting. He stands 5'10" and clocks in at 210 pounds, all of it the kind of muscle that scares the crap out of anybody with half a brain.)

Not only was Frank sort of a social outcast, he wasn't the greatest student. "I'm fully aware of where I stood on the intellectual spectrum: Right in the middle. I can learn what I want to learn, but when it comes to a topic I don't care about, it's a slog."

When it came to college, Frank and his parents were on the same page: nobody was interested in having him attend. Frank's parents didn't want him to go because they didn't have the money, and Frank didn't want to go because, well, he didn't want to go.

After graduation, Frank's parents weren't going to let him sit around the house for the next however-many-months, so they made him get a job. Work, however, was hard to come by in his small town, so he did odd jobs here and there: some construction work, some landscaping, some housecleaning. Nothing was interesting, he wasn't making any significant money, and his relationship with his parents was fraying at the edges. "It sucked," Frank told me, before closing up that line of discussion.

One morning about eight months later, Frank's father drove him to Pittsburgh, where they met with an Army recruiter. The interview process was far more difficult than Frank imagined. "I was in there for a couple of hours, and it was a challenge, but a *good* challenge. I was never a gung-ho, G.I. Joe type, but I do love my country, and after I spoke with the recruiter, I could see myself fighting for it."

Frank didn't find the Army's educational benefits particularly enticing. "I had zero interest in going to college, *zero*. I wasn't thinking too far ahead. It was like, 'Okay, this Army thing will keep me busy for a couple of years, and I'll figure it out from there.'"

He did his basic training at Fort Jackson in Columbia, South Carolina. Much to his surprise, he loved it. "There was a camaraderie that I'd never experienced. I was kind of a loner, and high school sucked, and I didn't have any brothers or sisters. I found people who were a lot like me, who were there because it was their best option. But there were other people who *were* gung-ho, G.I. Joe types, and they pushed the other guys—the guys like me—to try harder."

As is the case with most everything in his life, when Frank tried, he succeeded. "I kicked ass in basic training. As soon as I was done, I was sent to Afghanistan. And even though I was mentally and physical equipped to handle it, I was scared shitless."

Frank told me all about his two tours of Afghanistan, but I'm not allowed to write about it. Suffice it to say that we should all be thankful for what Frank and his fellow military men have done for this country.

After his second tour—which concluded in the summer of 2016—Frank landed a job at a government agency that I'm not allowed to name. "It wasn't a particularly exciting position, but after what I'd been through over the last eighteen months, *not particularly exciting* was awesome."

But Frank kicked butt at his not-particularly-exciting position and caught the eye of a recruiter from one of the government's alphabet soup law enforcement agencies. "The guy sent me a random email asking if I'd come in for an interview. That's not the kind of thing you say no to." The following week, Frank interviewed with five big government muckity-mucks, and was brought aboard the week after that. "It happened quick. My head was spinning."

As was the case in Frank's Government Job Number One, the new position wasn't particularly exciting, but there were some perks. "I got a shockingly nice raise, and my supervisor told me that if I crushed it, I'd get promoted quickly." Sure enough, he crushed it. Sure enough, he got promoted quickly.

As I'm writing this, Frank is waiting to hear about his *fourth* promotion, a supervisory position that he tells me, "could lead to really, really big things."

You see, during his time in Afghanistan, Frank learned a whole bunch of stuff that, you guessed it, I'm not allowed to discuss. But his skill set is highly specialized, and, given the opportunity, he'll do great things for the country. Frank's potential new job—which I'm 800 percent certain he'll get—comes with an excellent salary, a ton of responsibility, a move to New York City, and no end of challenges. It's the kind of job that Frank envisions doing for a long time. "I look around the office and see guys who have been there for ten, fifteen, twenty years. Some of them are kind of burnt out, and some of them are still psyched to be there, but there's that camaraderie I had in the field that I can't imagine finding in any other job."

In terms of his schooling—or lack thereof—Frank credits his father with making a terrific decision, even if it was just an instinctive one. "Dad wasn't in the military. For that matter nobody in our family had ever served. He once told me that he hauled me down to the recruiter's office because he couldn't think of anything else to do with me. I don't know where I'd be if he hadn't have done that."

While Frank has absolutely no regrets about skipping college, he's thrilled with the fact that he furthered his education. "Obviously the stuff I learned, I'd never learn at a regular school. Besides, I wasn't exactly what you'd call college material."

17

Let's say that you wanted to become a writer. Now let's say that the summer after you graduated high school, you wrote a novel. Now let's say that you showed the novel to a family friend who happened to be a literary agent. Now let's say that the literary agent showed the book to six different editors at six different publishing houses. Now let's say that those six editors all loved it, and their respective houses got into a bidding war as to who would acquire the rights. Now let's say that the bidding war ended with a three million dollar offer.

Now let's say there was an organization that told you, "Sorry, pal. You can't accept the offer until you go to college for a year."

That would be a teensy bit upsetting.

If you have a unique skill set—a skill set that is natural to you, a skill set that no college would be able to significantly improve upon—shouldn't you be able to immediately pursue your chosen profession?

Computer experts can do that, and have been able to do so for years. In an article from July 2011, *PC Magazine*'s Sara Yin told the story of several teenagers who turned their hacking skills into high-paying jobs, all without the benefit of four years of college. There was George Holtz who, after battling Sony in court over "unauthorized access" of his PlayStation 3, landed a computer security gig at Facebook. Then there was Peter Hajas, who, after launching an app that could break into smartphones, was hired by Apple—or what he called, "a fruit company." Then there was Jeff Moss, whose ability to hack into pretty much anything earned him a position on the U.S. Homeland Security Advisory Commission. Finally, there was Kevin Poulson, a notorious hacker, who, after serving five years in jail and paying fifty-six thousand dollars worth of fines, became a senior writer for *Wired* magazine.

Nobody told them they couldn't get right to work. But computers don't fall under the purview of the National Collegiate Athletic Association.

The NCAA is an organization that basically polices what student athletes can and can't do. It was founded in 1906, and some of their bylaws reflect their age. Their 2017–18 manual—which clocks in at a breezy 416 pages—breaks down everything from athlete recruiting, to infractions, to academic eligibility. It's an exhaustive tome that, when boiled down to its essence, tells us that, "An athlete can't play college sports unless he or she does what we say, when we say it."

It's a tad draconian.

And long. Really, really bloody long.

Now I'm not a sports guy, but one aspect of the NCAA rules that drives me batty—and I'm far from the only one—is professional basketball eligibility. The NCAA and the National Basketball Association believe that a teenager shouldn't be able to pursue a professional basketball career without attending one year of college, the reasoning being that an eighteen-year-old isn't ready for the rigors of the NBA without experiencing nine-plus months of higher education. This is called the "one and done" rule.

I get that, and I appreciate that. Professional sports, while a high-paying, high-profile job, is still a job, and any company wants their employees to be well-equipped to perform. The NBA brain trust feels that their workers need college seasoning.

Maybe that's true and maybe it's not, but in my humble opinion, if a basketball player—or *anybody*, for that matter—demonstrates they can perform any job at a high level, they should be allowed to perform that job whether they're eight, eighteen, or eighty.

To the NBA's credit, they're considering making changes. In February 2018, NBA Commissioner Adam Silver said, "We've had some meetings with the players' association where we've shared data on success rates of young players coming into the league. We've talked a lot about youth development in terms of whether we should be getting involved in some of these young players even earlier than when they come into college."

But Silver then qualified that by adding, "On the other hand, I think the question for the league is, in terms of their ultimate success, are we better off intersecting with them a little bit younger? And there is also recognition that for some of these elite players, there is no question that they can perform in the NBA at eighteen years old."

Interestingly enough, two notable individual sports—tennis and golf—have super-lenient age requirements. You can join the United States Tennis Association at the age of fourteen, while the Professional Golf Association allows you to jump in at eighteen. And that's a good thing. If the USTA had stringent age restrictions, then-sixteen-year-old Serena Williams wouldn't have had the opportunity to upset Monica Seles and win the 1997 Ameritech Cup Chicago. If the PGA were hardasses about ages, Rory McIlroy wouldn't have been able to earn over ten million dollars before the age of twenty-two.

If you can do the job, you should be allowed to do the job, regardless of what the job is.

There was a time when the NBA allowed players to jump straight from high school to the pros, and the jumps were often wildly successful. LeBron James, Kobe Bryant, Kevin Garnett, and Amar'e Stoudemire wouldn't have gotten better at basketball in college. If you want to support you and your family by playing a sport, nobody should be able to keep you from doing so.

18

Listen, I can spout facts and figures about college all day long. I can give you lists and examples. I can stand on my soapbox and scream until I'm purple in the face. But what it boils down to—and yes, I know I've discussed this throughout the book, but it bears repeating—is passion.

Passion is the glue that holds everything together: your family, your marriage, your career, your house, your dinner, *everything*. Without passion, life is a windowless room with gray paint and no furniture.

You have to be passionate. You have to believe in yourself. You have to be confident. You have to be fearless. You have to go for it.

If all of those emotions are properly attuned, if you're in touch with the best part of yourself, you'll have the ability to make the most difficult decisions, decisions like whether or not to introduce college into your or your family's life.

There are a whole lot of societal forces that push children towards higher education: the promise of more money, the promise of a better life, the promise of four years of freedom. Sometimes those promises come to fruition, and sometimes they don't—and I'd like to think that if you've stuck with me for this many pages, you'll now agree that since none of these promises are anything close to guaranteed, it's well worth internal and external examination as to whether college is worth it.

Consider the investment. Consider the uncertainty. Consider the inflexibility. Consider the inconsistency.

But mostly, consider the children.

This decision—this momentous decision—isn't about the parents. It's all about the teenager about to enter the adult world. Check that: it's all about the teenager entering the adult world in the manner that's best for *them*.

It's a complex issue with a simple solution, if only because you have two answers: yes or no.

If it's a yes—if the kid in question is going to enroll in college—make certain it's the right college. And if it's not the right one, don't be afraid to switch or call it quits.

If it's a no—if the kid in question is going immediately into the work force, military or is heading to a trade school—make certain you have all the facts. Facts about the child, facts about the job; facts about the trade.

You have to be prepared to put it all on the line. You have to be prepared to endure hardship. You have to be prepared to overcome obstacles. You have to be prepared to do all of those things, otherwise, it's just not going to happen for you.

And because you're in America, you can do it. You can make it happen—on your own terms.

Abraham Lincoln, the ultimate American, was entirely self-taught. He didn't go to elementary school, didn't go to middle school, didn't go to high school, didn't go to college; nothing.

Everything he learned, he taught himself. He figured it out himself.

I also figured it out myself. Even today—even though I make a living speaking in front of crowds—I like to pull out my iPod, which is full of speeches from Winston Churchill, and Barack Obama, and JFK, and Ronald Reagan, and every single major political figure I've ever found inspirational. What I learned from those speeches—what I learned from watching *YouTube* videos of these men—are things I'd never learn in college.

I want the people reading this book—who are mostly going to be Americans—to understand how lucky they are to be in this country. And the fact that they're here should make the college decision easier, because this is a country where dreams are precious, where dreams are encouraged, where you're not laughed at for having a non-traditional goal.

I have never, ever been excited or aroused by the thought of owning an airplane, or having a fleet of yachts, or filling my garage with cars that cost five hundred thousand dollars. Those things have never interested me. I have always wanted to leave a legacy. What's always animated me was the prospect of history in the books referencing my name and the work that I did. What sustains me, what my dream is, is having my grandchildren, and great-grandchildren, and great-great-grandchildren reading about me in their school text books.

Yes, that may sound boastful, but that's just me being me. For as long as I can remember, people have told me they think I'm arrogant. Even back when I was a kid, teachers told my parents that I was over the top. (Admittedly, it was probably warranted.) My father always said to me to never be afraid to be called arrogant because in 99.9 percent of the cases, self-confidence is perceived as arrogance, and people are threatened by self-confidence. Because if you're confident and they're not, that makes them feel insecure, and the way for them to simultaneously damage you and make themselves feel better is by calling you arrogant.

Now, I have always had a supreme self-confidence in my abilities, who I am, and what I believe and so people want to call that arrogant? That's their prerogative.

But I don't think you can pursue and achieve the American Dream without a touch of arrogance and a whole heap of self-confidence. When I look back at every scary decision I've had to make, when I look back to every time I was staring into the abyss, when I look back on every time I doubted myself, and when I look back at every time that I've triumphed, it's always boiled down to fearlessness. I've always been prepared to endure anything: the good, the bad, the ugly, and everything in between.

And you know why? Because I knew I was prepared to out-hustle, out-hit, out-tackle, out-weigh any opponent.

You can't take the kind of leap of faith necessary to begin your professional life without a college degree if you're full of fear, doubt, and uncertainty. Not that those things aren't natural—everybody is scared of something...or several somethings—but you've got to overcome these fears, because if you don't overcome them, you're not going to fulfill your dreams. And if you don't fulfill your dreams, no one outside of your immediate circle of friends and family is going to remember who you are. You're not going to leave a legacy.

You have to have testicular fortitude. You can't have the spine of a jellyfish. You have to be one million percent committed. The American Dream will not come to you. You have to come to the American Dream, and you have to come prepared.

So let's make sure that every American child knows they are not limited by their first language or last name, or by their color or gender or sexual orientation. Let's make sure that every American child can dream. Let's make sure that every American child understands the foundations of our country. Let's make sure every American child has a heart beating for America. Let's make sure that today's child is willing and able to pass on Americanism to tomorrow's child.

America's foundational principles aren't suspect; they're special. I want American children to understand that America is not perfect, but it is the best thing we have. I want young Americans to know that initiative and confidence go much further here than anywhere else. I want young Americans to know that when they were born in the United States of America, they won the lottery of life. I want them to believe in competition. I want them to believe in winning. I want them to aspire to greatness and disdain mediocrity. I want them to be proud of who they are and where they come from. I want them to know there is no limit on individual human potential and no limit to what America can achieve.

Dear reader, I want you to be bold, to veer away from vanilla and into the chocolate.

I want you to lead an interesting life, to not be a sheep, to not be the unfortunate soul who goes to work because they *have* to.

I want you to live your life for your eulogy, not for your résumé.

I want you to be red hot on the American Dream. And if you think you need college to get to that level, you, my friend, are sadly mistaken. Success, potential, and dreams are all inside of your heart, not inside a textbook.

ACKNOWLEDGMENTS

When I was a little boy, I loved reading. In fact, it was as though books defied gravity—I simply couldn't put them down! It got to the point where I would find myself deliberately testing the limits of what was allowed at home. No matter where I was—at my parents' house in Australia, or with my grandparents in Germany or Greece—I had my nose in a book, day and night, night and day. Thing is, nighttime meant bedtime, and bedtime was non-negotiable. Lights out. Time to go to sleep. Reading session over.

But as soon as any adult had disappeared from sight, I would immediately reach under my pillow and pull out the small flashlight I'd hidden in my pillowcase and continue reading. This, of course, had a detrimental effect on my eyes (leading to the need for glasses), but it was well worth it.

I still love to read and do so at any opportunity possible, but one of the unavoidable realities of entrepreneurship is having less time for the pleasure. I mention this because I wonder often what nine-year-old Nick Adams—the kid with the flashlight in one hand and the reading material in the other—would think of having written his own book. It's both intoxicating and humbling.

I thank God every day for America, a unique, exceptional, and extraordinary nation, an idea and culture that has afforded me the opportunity to achieve the dreams I've had in my heart. As Esteban Blanco, my close friend and fellow immigrant says, "The only thing I can't be is President. Everything else is up for grabs, because I live in America."

To all the organizations across the country that used my services and gave me a chance to ply my craft—thank you for giving me my shot.

One of my favorite places in American is my adopted home state of Texas. Being a Texan is a remarkable privilege. I say to students all the time, if you're a native American, you've won the lottery of life, and if you were born in, or live in Texas, you hit the jackpot!

The men who inspired this book are those I refer to as American originals, men such as Abraham Lincoln, Benjamin Franklin, the Wright Brothers, John D. Rockefeller, Walt Disney, Steve Jobs, and Bill Gates. These innovators are rare, but far less so in America. This is, in large part, because traditionally, Americans don't lean on the government to get things done. (Ideally, the government stays out of their way.) Americans instead rely on their own ingenuity. In America, the only limit to your ambition is your own imagination.

And then there are the individuals who made this book possible. First, I must thank my beautiful wife, Sadie for supporting my vision and work with love and affection. Her quiet grace and dignity strengthen me. Thank you for loving and caring for me.

Four years ago, I was introduced to Anthony Ziccardi of Post Hill Press, and it was one of the best things that ever happened to me. The entire team, with particular mention to Alan Goldsher, was stellar.

To my koumbaro, Evan Angelopoulos, for now being family.

To my parents, for giving me unending support and always putting me first. Your inspiration can never be justified with ink and the tears that would do justice will flow for as long as I have breath. Thank you for who you are and who you have allowed me to become. I know I am your legacy, and that means more to me than you will ever know. I love you.

To my Australian friends Ange, Mick, Jimmy, Nick, and Pete, for always being there.

To Sanjay. Our conversations and your counsel remain integral to making sense of a complicated world.

To the many others who have crossed my path, and validated my choices, I salute you: John Rogitz, Don Gobin, Jim Volpe, Chad Carlson, Steve Cortes, Chris Betts, David Prager, Robert Krueger, Mike Hornbuckle, The Sargent Family, Brian Kilmeade, Joe and Nancy Wemhoff, Donna Belton, Barry Schlech, Gerald and Diane Haddock, Mike and Ellen Handa, Don and Phillip Huffines, The Clegg Family, Parker Rosenberger, Vince Benedetto, Tony and Sherrie McKnight, Donnie Sumner, Bill O'Reilly, Austin Ferrer, Desiree Thompson Sayle, Joy Greggo, Adele Ward, The Pitzers, John and Andi Bos, The Dobski Family, Stuart Varney, Debbie and Chris Phelan, George and Joan Voneiff, James Crocker, Uncle George, Jim and Joanie Pikl, Anne Schockett, Deanne Tate, Congressman Gus Bilirakis, Rick Green, Lee and Caroline Wetherington, and Joe and Sherry Hurt.

Finally, I'm proud of my Greek Orthodox faith, and beyond all, I thank God for preserving my life when I should never have lived.